8 Strategies for
Successful
Step-Parenting

8 Strategies for

Successful
Step-Parenting

Nadir Baksh, Psy.D.
& Laurie Murphy, Ph.D.

HOHM PRESS
Prescott, Arizona

Cover design: Adi Zuccarello: www.adizuccarello.com

Layout and Interior Design: Zac Parker, Kadak Graphics, Prescott, Arizona

Library of Congress Cataloging-in-Publication Data

Baksh, Nadir.
8 strategies for successful step-parenting / Nadir Baksh & Laurie Murphy.
    p. cm.
Includes bibliographical references and index.
ISBN 978-1-935387-08-4 (trade pbk. : alk. paper)
1. Stepparents. 2. Stepfamilies. 3. Parenting. 4. Remarriage. I. Murphy, Laurie. II. Title. III. Title: Eight strategies for successful step-parenting.
HQ759.92.B357 2010
649'.1--dc22
                                    2009054207

HOHM PRESS
P.O. Box 2501
Prescott, AZ 86302
800-381-2700
http://www.hohmpress.com

This book was printed in the U.S.A. on recycled, acid-free paper using soy ink.

CONTENTS

DEDICATION

We are constantly reminded that children's lives are shaped more by the individuals with whom they are linked than by genetics or world events. Each of us teaches lessons, positively or negatively, that impact generations. Children are our immediate future. This book is dedicated to step-parents everywhere, whose selfless devotion and sacrifices have changed the course of their children's lives. Jose Gonzalez was one of those people.

ACKNOWLEDGMENTS

Writing a book is serious business. The written word carries enormous weight; consequently these words must be carefully chosen. We are aware of the individual influences that have come together to help us formulate our ideas, shape our philosophies, and believe in our work with all our heart. We acknowledge these influences.

We have learned about human behavior from those individuals right under our noses; for us it was the carefree innocence of our children that taught us (rather than the other way around), unaware of the lessons they were giving. Nothing, we discovered, is more filled with wonder than a wobbly toddler, more willing to learn than an enthusiastic student, more defiant than a rebellious teenager, and more resilient than the human spirit of the child. We acknowledge our children.

We work in a profession that offers us firsthand glimpses into unraveling families, splintered marriages, and hopeful second chances; and close contact with adults who strive to successfully blend families, sometimes against all odds. We are always amazed by their tenacity, their angst and their ability to right themselves even when their world tilts. We are proud to be a part of our clients' lives and congratulate them on their accomplishments.

This book is born after a very long labor; it has been meticulously nursed by our managing editor, Regina Sara Ryan, who believed that we could do better, and would not allow us to stop writing until we had. The entire Hohm Press team has always stepped into the background as they pushed us into the limelight; we could not have done it without them.

Most of all we are humbled by Divine Intervention, placing us where we need to be when we need to be there.

INTRODUCTION

This is a book about step-parenting. It is also a book about cooperation, understanding, teamwork, forgiveness, account-ability and love.

This book is for you:

- If you are already a step-parent, or you are soon to become one
- If you are a biologic parent who is about to remarry or has remarried
- If you have been happily married but experienced the untimely death of your spouse and have now decided to remarry.

We have tried to exclude no one. Whether you are in an orthodox or unorthodox family structure, if the circumstances that have brought you to our book include the goal of success-fully blending your new family, whether you have ever parented or never parented before, we have the compass to guide you on the road to happy and successful step-parenting.

This book covers 8 Strategies designed to help you create a realistic vision of *who you are*, and where you would *like to be* within your new "blended family"—a term that applies to the combination of children and adults from previous marriages, but also includes all other pertinent members of the prior family unit who will continue to impact the current family. These indi-viduals include grandparents, aunts, uncles, cousins, close family friends and even the family dog; in other words, any person (or pet) who has played an integral role in the lives of the children, and who will continue to be important in their lives.

Each chapter will build upon the previous ones, incorporating questions such as:

- Are my expectations realistic?
- Can I achieve them?
- What type of emotional support can I expect from my spouse?
- What is the significance of each person's role in the new family dynamics?

Your relationship to your partner's former spouse (or your partner's relationship to *your* former spouse) will be addressed, since this person is integral to the confusion around, and the solution to, much of the turmoil surrounding your step-children's behavior, and how this turmoil can be lessened.

8 Strategies for Successful Step-Parenting especially recognizes the importance of your role as a step-parent, and the sacrifices you have chosen to make in order to successfully blend your new family. As with any endeavor, there will be some bumps in your journey. Throughout the book, we will stress the importance of asking for assistance when you come up against a major roadblock or a "Dead End." We believe there is a resolution to every problem, and will offer guidance as you confront your difficulties head-on, and find the joy you initially envisioned when you agreed to become a step-parent.

Vignettes of thirty-one families and individuals are included throughout the book. These are based on the true experiences of our clients (modified to protect identity), and hopefully will serve to clarify each of the strategies presented here. Although these stories may not be specific to your predicaments, they will surely highlight aspects of a situation you have gone through alone, or issues that you too have misunderstood. Your circumstances are unique to your family, but we trust that all our readers have the common denominator of wanting things to be better. And we know they can be!

Step-parenting is serious business that can be enormously rewarding both to you and your step-children. This book will assist you in gaining insight and understanding into your own expertise with relationships and parenting, as well as with the hidden pitfalls that can hamper the success of any blended family. It is written not only for those individuals who are step-parents, but also for the biological parent-partners whose guidance, input and support is vital to the cohesiveness of the family unit. Both of you need to work hand in hand in a true partnership, but this good intention is often misdirected unless both partners are given ample information.

We have organized a wealth of experience into these eight necessary step-parenting strategies. A strategy is a plan of action to pave the road as you attain your goals. Every goal is unique and completely within your grasp. Enjoy your journey!

What This Book Will Cover

Strategy #1: *Know Who You Are: Take A Personal Inventory* will address the foundational issues of:
- Defining your new role for yourself
- Learning more about yourself
- Assessing your potential strengths and weaknesses as a step-parent.

Here we will encourage you to awaken your senses as you sample our Personal Inventory, Sentence Completion Assignment. We created this tool to help you gain insight as you become acquainted with your true self.

Strategy #2: *Examine Your Expectations* deals with various issues ranging from dating to marriage. These include:
- Assessing realistic and unrealistic expectations
- What to do when children say they "hate" the new partner

- How to deal with feelings of disloyalty toward biologic children
- Incorporating honesty as a foundation within the
  family
- Juggling your roles of intimate partner and new step-
  parent.

Questions addressed in this chapter include:

- When to tell your child about a new partner
- What to expect when you meet your partner's children for the first time
- How to separate prior biologic parenting skills from
  your new role as step-parent
- How to gain confidence when you don't have prior
  parenting skills
- How to identify and separate positive feelings for children from negative assessment of their behavior.

Strategy #3: *Use the Hierarchy Ladder: A Short Course in Family Dynamics* shows you how to cope with step-parenting challenges while keeping your marriage fresh and your household under control. These action steps include:

- Understanding the family hierarchy
- Appreciating the timing in family dynamics
- Drafting and using a Behavior-Consequence Chart
- Prioritizing which issues should *always* be enforced
- Establishing protection for each member of your
  family.

Strategy #4: *"Make Nice" With the Former Spouse* deals with difficult issues that may arise between you and the former spouse. We know it is challenging to deal with insecurities arising from jealousy or intimidation; and we know it is vital to establish a relationship of open and honest communication with the former spouse, in order to help step-children bridge the gap.

This chapter offers pro-active advice and answers questions like: When should I call attention to the different parenting philosophies in each home?

Strategy #5: *Create a Parenting Partnership* will emphasize that your parent-partner's job cannot be minimized. This chapter offers advice to encourage and applaud parent-partner support, and will help you identify those behaviors (in yourself and your partner) that need modification as you transition into your roles. It addresses such questions as:

- What gender differences relate to parenting expectations?
- Why do men and women communicate differently?
- How do my preconceived expectations sabotage my new partner's role?

Strategy #6: *Respect the Past as You Create the Future.* With this chapter you will be well on your way to tossing out old insecurities and embracing both old and new memories. We will also consider:

- The importance of blending traditions, and incorporating religious differences
- Finding room for old and new family photographs
- Wedding day plans that respect all parties
- Housing arrangements for all types of blended families, including residential and non-residential children
- Honoring extended family members.

Strategy #7: *Never Underestimate Your Importance!* is about appreciating your importance in the family. This chapter is our favorite section of the book. It contains one woman's true story as she learns the meaning of the love of a step-parent. In it, she attempts to complete unfinished business, writing a eulogy to her beloved step-father on the first anniversary of his untimely death.

Read this story any time, and many times, particularly when you need encouragement in this challenging task of step-parenting.

Strategy #8: *Get the Help You Need* deals with difficult issues that may arise for even the most well-intentioned step-parents—issues that you can't or shouldn't deal with alone. What if you are unable to bond with your step-children? What if you decide to terminate your marriage? What if your children are seriously suffering?

This chapter also contains a Resource Guide that you can refer to all along the way. Here you will find helpful books, websites, and numbers to call for counseling help.

❖

As therapists, we have worked with families just like yours for more than twenty-seven years. Aside from *8 Strategies to Successful Step-Parenting*, we have also written *In The Best Interest of the Child, A Manual for Divorcing Parents* and *You Don't Know Anything, A Manual for Parenting Your Teenager.* Our intimate involvement with our clients have offered us a hands-on approach to the process of well-balanced step-parenting dynamics, not only from the perspective of blending strangers into bonded relationships, but in recognizing the importance of the former partners and their impact either positively or negatively on the blended family. We are confident that we are able to assist you to gain confidence and control just as we have helped other step-parents and families to do the same.

We want you to succeed, and with very little effort, you will. Regardless of your own unique situation, each of you brings valuable experiences to the table. You have been raised with philosophies that may resemble others' on the surface, but underneath you have a treasure-trove of experiences, talents, memories, and wisdom that have been handed down for generations within your family. As a new or prospective step-parent, each of you, regardless of your talents and experiences, feels apprehension, anxiety, and concern that you are undertaking a new role for which you are not fully prepared. This is square one! Regardless of wealth, education, family background or wishful thinking, we all begin with little more than a firm intention. Whether we are employed by a five-star company or are temporarily unemployed makes no essential difference to our step-children; what does matter is our genuine desire to be a loving, contributing member of this family. Step-parenting is as fundamentally different and equally as rewarding as anything you have ever done, or will ever do again.

On a more personal note, we (Nadir and Laurie) also share a blended family; ours is comprised of a single man without children married to a mother of four children. We have experienced first hand the triumphs and the disappointments that come with venturing into the uncharted territory of this unique parenting situation. This allows us to offer you not only professional but also personal advice that has worked both with our clients and in our own blended family. These strategies will work for you too.

STRATEGY #1
Know Who You Are:
Take a Personal Inventory

Blending families is difficult work. Your role in this new family is pivotal, and your impact will be so vital that your importance should never be underestimated. You have actually been awarded a great opportunity to change the course of children's lives   by the example you lead, the love you offer and the wisdom you possess. You have joined your new family at the exact moment at which they need you.

Some facts may help you to understand what step-parenting is all about. Today's statistics reveal that as much as 65 percent of all marriages end in divorce, and among those divorced couples more than 50 percent are parents. Among those divorced parents, many if not most will remarry. That means that you are joining an overwhelming number of adults in our society who have chosen to become step-parents.

Signing up for your new journey already offers some insight into who you are, and in this chapter you will be invited to explore this issue more thoroughly in preparation for your new job. From our perspective, a step-parent is not only a parent through marriage, but someone who is not afraid of taking risks. You are that someone. Being responsible for the day- to-day physical, emotional and spiritual care of someone else's children takes a lot of guts! It also takes persistence, optimism, focus, and love for your new partner, enough to commit yourself to his or her children. Step-parenting in due time will prove its own reward.

Qualifications

Some of you may wonder whether you possess the necessary qualifications to take on such an enormous task. Most likely, you turned a blind eye to the prospects of step-parenting during the initial phase of your courtship, just like so many of your counterparts. Yet, even as you began to comprehend the total picture of what was in store for you, you didn't waver. We believe that if you have a willingness to learn, an ability to remain patient during chaos, an uncanny knack for searching out the positives in negative situations, and the genuine desire to be a part of your step-children's lives, you are well on your way.

If you are willing to love your step-children even when some of their behavior makes them unlovable, you more than meet the qualifications of a step-parent. This is not to minimize the task at hand. There will be times when your resolve will be tested and when self-doubt will make you wonder why you even wanted to be responsible for what seems to be a thankless situation. But, isn't that the nature of parenting in general?

When your confidence is shaken, when you feel unappreciated, when you're emotionally wrung out, it will be most important to remember who you are. Learning your strengths and weaknesses through a Personal Inventory, as this chapter suggests, will be your lifeline.

We appreciate that many of you come into your step-children's lives as an outsider. Unlike their biologic parent, you have no sacrosanct union of DNA and genetics to lean on, no magic key to unlock the "circle"—that bond they've already established.

Whether you are a learned person or uneducated, whether you have discovered the cure for cancer or you work on a factory line, you enter your new family without credentials. They will be given to you only as you earn them, judged by children who will often be unfair in their decisions. During the "probation period" (we suggest at least six months to one year) your qualifications will be called on the carpet not only by your step-children, but certainly by the other biologic parent. Nothing will be off-limits, including your appearance, personality, and parenting skills. You will have to pass tests for which you have not studied, from administrators who lack credentials, and your "report card" will fall short of your own standards.

No one said this undertaking would be easy; in fact, even among childish career choices such as, "When I grow up I want to be an astronaut who lives on the moon," or "I want to be Spiderman and save the good people," it is unlikely that any child anywhere in the universe uttered the words, "When I grow up I want to be a step-parent." Yet here you are. You may already have children of your own, or this may be your first time around, but "inexperience" is not always synonymous with "disadvantage." In fact, it is unfair for anyone (including yourself) to imply that you are an unlikely candidate to be a successful step-parent. We are all the sum total of our experiences, and those experiences allow each of you to bring forth your wisdom and knowledge, all equally valuable in life lessons. In any parenting situation no two individuals will share identical philosophies. Although they may differ, with some being more functionally appropriate than others, they all contain insights, information, and wisdom that have been handed down for generations. In some ways, inexperience may be your advantage: it allows an individual to ask for help, research information, and be more willing to continually evaluate his or her progress.

Often a step-parent's self-doubt implicates them without cause. That line of thinking, while often unrealistic, is destructive nonetheless, and if not kept in check takes on a life of its own.

As you'll read in the story below, Stacey's self-doubt almost cost her marriage.

Stacey's Story

Stacey was convinced the only solution to her blended family's problems was for her to file for divorce; she was absolutely certain that she was the sole reason that her step-son's poor grades hinged on his inability to adjust to his new step-mother. In actuality, step-son Matt hadn't really reacted one way or another when his father Dick remarried; it was true that Matt was introverted at home, but with his peers he was gregarious and fun-loving, behavior not at all uncommon with teenagers. He had just celebrated his sixteenth birthday and his hormones were in full swing; he was coming into his own, but some of those characteristics included risk-taking behavior and a sense of edginess and arrogance.

Dick voiced his shock at the change in his son, but rather than attributing it to teenage behavior, he left his statements open-ended; Stacey filled in the blanks silently. She believed that Matt's difficulties were a direct result of her inadequate step-parenting, and that in order to save him from a life of poor choices, she would have to sacrifice her marriage.

When the family arrived in therapy, it was easy to see what was going on in the family dynamics; in truth, Dick was emotionally absent when it came to solution seeking, leaving most of the responsibility to Stacey. While he busied himself at work, staying later and later hours, she was at home trying to rein-in her adventurous step-son. It was no wonder that she let the brunt of "blame" fall upon her shoulders. We helped the parents make a Behavior-Consequence chart (see Strategy #3) for Matt, and enlisted Dick's help in enforcing the consequences. Once Stacey was freed of the sole burden, and Matt quickly realized there were consequences to his behavior, the family found its way back to some harmony; the rest will come as Matt matures.

Like Stacy, everyone has fears, doubts and trepidation when they make changes. This is normal. As you learn about yourself, acknowledging both strengths and weaknesses, you will have a more realistic understanding of what to expect, both from yourself and from your spouse.

All Experience Is Not Equal

An individual with lots of parenting experience may believe that step-parenting is simply an extension of biologic parenting. That notion could not be farther from the truth. Step-parenting is uniquely different from biologic parenting in so many ways, the least of which is that you are meeting children at various stages of development for which you have had no input. These step-children are already biologically and emotionally encoded, and in ways that may vary dramatically from the children you already have. Before you ever set eyes on them, your step-children have already been raised under a different set of conditions, biases and expectations. Certainly your wisdom and experiences will help to shape them from here on, but, unlike a newborn whose world is shaped almost entirely by your personal modeling, imprinting and influences, step-children cannot discard learned information and begin anew.

A biological parent has no reason to worry about "winning" the affection of their child. A step-parent will! Regardless of parental credentials, a biologic child accepts parents as they are, basking in their parent's attributes and learning to "protect" and defend any parental flaws. For a biologic parent there is no examination to pass, no report card to be signed, no external scrutiny to be worried about. In many ways, biologic parents are given a "free pass" with an anticipated successful outcome as the bond between natural parents and their children becomes stronger every day, with each adapting to the others' personality traits, strengths and weaknesses, talents and shortcomings. This bond breathes, growing together and apart in a rhythmical, genetically-orchestrated interdependence. This bond may be so tightly formed that a new step-parent may despair of ever finding an opening into this inner sanctum.

Once again, experienced with children or not, your job is a challenging one. Your strongest resources will be your own self-esteem and self-knowledge. Strategy #1 is to take the time to learn about you.

Martha's Story

Martha walked into our counseling office unannounced; she had never been a patient of ours before, but heard that we had experience helping with family situations. "I have a mess on my hands" she cried. "I love my new husband but I have no idea why I thought I could be a step-mother to his children. I don't know what I'm doing and I think they know I don't know what I'm doing!"

We allowed Martha to express the same sentiments in various ways for the next fifteen minutes. It was apparent that she very much wanted to be a wife and step-mother, but had no experience with either role. The courtship and wedding seemed so romantic that she never stopped to imagine how the rest of her life would play out. After only two weeks, she suddenly doubted her ability to give advice, parent, set boundaries, keep her marriage fresh, go to work, make the dinner, and care for her own elderly parents. In her state of mind it was clear that she was not only overwhelmed with the day to day realities, but that she had begun her new role based upon a faulty foundation of low self-esteem and insecurity. We knew that Martha was going to be just fine, but first she would have to spend some time on introspection and clarification. With our coaxing she was willing to take some deep breaths on the spot. She also accepted our word that with some information and application she would master her anxieties and gain the necessary confidence to make her original dreams a reality.

Martha was about to discover that before she could become a confident step-parent, she needed a grasp on successful adulthood—a condition that hinges directly upon the contents of her emotional suitcase. As her suitcase was "emptied" through identification and resolution of past experiences, her worry, anxiety, fear and faulty perceptions could be released. Like Martha, we hope that you will take the time to open your suitcase and begin sifting through those issues that are causing you anger, insecurity and any other obstacles that stand in your way as a successful step-parent.

Who Are You?

In our practice, one of the questions we like to ask is, "Who do you think you are?" This question renders most people speechless for a few moments, as they fixate on adjectives to describe themselves best. Certainly our clients think they know who they are. Yet almost all of them quickly discover that they do not know themselves that well. Believing (or wishing) that they are one person, they later find out (or secretly know) that they are quite another. Only those introspective individuals who have made the time to "research"—directly addressing and living with—the eternal and often illusive question, "Who am I?" can really have a deeper understanding of themselves.

Martha believed she was incapable of handling more than one project or issue at a time, because her mother always "rescued" her when things became overwhelming. Since her mother died (one year before we met her), Martha had stumbled through her life, intellectually advantaged but emotionally stifled. It was as if when her mother died Martha's ability to cope died as well. After taking a Personal Inventory like the one we offer you later in this chapter, Martha became acquainted with herself for the first time. She saw that, while her strengths were always present, they were overshadowed by her mother's concern that Martha might not make the right decision. Consequently, she allowed mother to make all her decisions. Martha soon understood that stumbling and even falling were a necessary part of life. We learn from our experience, and those falls are what propel the next success.

Shaping Self-Esteem

How could someone who wakes up with themselves each day not know their own strengths and weaknesses? As we retrace a common sequence of how self-esteem and self-understanding is created here, we hope you will see aspects of your story. At the same time, realize that this sequence is applicable to the children you are embracing, both your biologic and your step-sons or daughters.

During children's formative years they take their cues from their parents—whose comments may range from their offspring's exceptional intelligence to their clumsy stupidity. These comments serve to reinforce a child's already self-centered preoccupation with themselves and their needs; or, in neglect or emotional abuse, the comments may infer laziness, ignorance and an inability to be valued. There is nothing to contradict these opinions and, therefore, whether Mom and Dad are disappointed by their child's presumed poor behavior, or astounded by their child's advanced learning skills, the child is willing to adapt these opinions as their own.

Self-esteem is born in the nursery. From one extreme to the other, a child may be considered an unconfident, non-motivated burden to the family, or treated as a precious gift swaddled in a blanket of exaggerated accolades that insulate the simple, real truths of his or her essential beauty and uniqueness. These parental beliefs, once adopted, begin to shape the pathway toward adulthood. Neither belief can survive without contamination from the outside world. Either way, the perfect identity of innocence is marred by harsh comments or embarrassed compliments, until the confusion of what a child believes they are is overshadowed by what others believe.

Even among the most self-assured children, it is not long before school mates and teachers begin to reshape the perception of perfection. Day by day, character flaws are identified and illuminated by other children who find it amusing to belittle others for a quick laugh. Thus, inhibitions are borne and, suddenly, spontaneous dancing becomes a careful walk, while emotions are quietly placed behind a blank mask. It doesn't take much humiliation for a child to quickly recognize that to avoid being the brunt of jokes it is necessary to follow and mimic those children who have been deemed "popular." Until maturity, children will shed their identity in order to preserve their dignity, always striving to remain above the invisible place where unpopular souls are forced to live out their school days as outcasts.

Think back on your own experiences. If you were popular, you know it only took one misstep to thrust you into the pit of the misfortunate; if you were among the unpopular, you may not have dared focusing attention on yourself by participating in class, or by joining an after school activity. Rather, it was often much safer to begin the emotional carpentry of building protective walls against the whispered insults that echoed in school corridors. The ages from five through eighteen or twenty are often so harrowing to many young adults that they feel as though they are treading water in the deep end of the ocean, barely able to stay afloat, always worrying about drowning.

Whatever allowed you to be fun-loving and carefree as a toddler may have been long discarded for self-preservation during the adolescent and young adult years. While some, of course, had the nerve, or dumb luck, to follow their dreams and develop their identity regardless of the opinions of others, those people are few and far between. The rest were more likely to muddle through, allowing life to pull them along, rather than vice versa.

In retrospect, the challenges faced from ages twenty to thirty can still send shivers down the most stoic spine. Ready or not, life thrusts its way in, often uninvited, with responsibilities. There were children to bear and raise, bills to pay, budgets to balance, relationships to make and break, marriages and divorces, job interviews and evaluations, until any remaining semblance of spontaneity and impulsivity was nothing but a faded memory. These were not the times to take time off to get acquainted with your identity; these were the times when everyone else's needs demanded to be met, with little regard for your own.

Most individuals have become the sum total of what their parents think they are, what they believed their classmates believed, what their academic accomplishments or failures depicted, what their girlfriends said behind their backs, what their boyfriends told their friends about them in the locker rooms. Their choice of mates, houses and neighborhoods have determined their worth, and social calendars their popularity. The truth is that most people go through life with little or no idea of who they are without someone else telling them.

Embracing Your Unique Identity

Becoming a step-parent means that you are going to have to walk boldly into your new role with confidence, forgiving yourself for past mistakes, applauding your achievements thus far, and, regardless of the speed bumps you are likely to encounter as you and your step-children learn about each other, do your best to stay aware of the ways you allow someone else to define you. Your identity is unique. Good, bad or otherwise, you need to own it before you can improve upon it or delight in it. You are not just someone's wife or husband, someone's friend or parent, a good cook or a poor housekeeper. You have hopes and dreams, you have innate talents, you see the world in a way unique only to you. There are no rules to being an individual, with the exception that individuality means that you cannot be the clone of someone else and expect your spirit to survive.

Before you lose yourself in the mix of children and step-children, spouses and former spouses, external family members through bloodlines and marital lines, you can move toward being centered in yourself. Once you have become familiar with who you are, who you have become, and who you strive to be, you will be surprised at the new-found confidence that accompanies this knowledge. You are less likely to waver when you feel overwhelmed; you will not be so desperate to fit in to your new family that you give away all your values; and you will not be so insecure that you cling to old habits that never really worked anyway. This is your moment to shine. This is your moment to take the step into adulthood where your stories, your laugh, your intellect, your wisdom and even your blunders are welcomed.

Taking a Personal Inventory

The checklist that follows will allow you to take a personal inventory of your strengths and weaknesses. This inventory is made by you, not anyone else, and for you, as you are now. It consists of unfinished phrases designed to make you think. Obviously they cannot be answered fully in the small space on the page, nor completed in one minute, or perhaps even one day. We suggest that you copy these unfinished sentences into a journal or notebook where you can write about them at length. Even if you don't write out your answers, we hope you will think about them as you drive, as you cook, as you walk the dog. As you work with them, the truth will come.

The checklist is not all inclusive. Begin our list and then add specifics of your own, keeping in mind that your life is dynamic not stagnant, that your evolving life will not answer the questions in the same manner next year or perhaps even next month. We are growing, and with growth comes insight. Every experience is a life lesson from which you continue to carve out your path. Keep moving, take the journey, don't stand still and let the elements beat you down. You decide what to keep in your life and what to discard; you decide those things that need some fine tuning and those things that are just fine.

Before you begin, if you make yourself a promise not to divulge your answers to another living soul, you will free yourself from the opinions of others and the fear of external judgment, which will allow you to speak (or write or think about) the truth. And as someone once very adeptly said, "The truth will set you free."

My Personal Inventory

Part I

Instructions: Here are some guidelines as you edit your own list.

- If you chose not to answer some sentences, or add in others, please do.
- Remember, this inventory is unique and personal to you. It is meant to acquaint you with the person you are and the person you may strive to become.
- It is best to complete this inventory within a few days.
- Some questions may conjure memories of days gone by, be they positive or negative, and you may feel compelled to write more than a few sentences. That's good!

- Some unfinished sentences can remain unfinished, especially if you are not ready to face some issues and the feelings they may elicit.
- Please make note of the sentences you choose to skip at this time, as they may be covering unfinished business. You can always go back to them at a later time, when you are ready.

I believe I am a good person because...
I believe I am a good friend because...
I have never really learned to roll with the punches because...
I am without anxiety only when...
I don't believe that people will like me if they actually knew...
One of the secrets I have been carrying for a long time is...
I am ashamed of...
One of my saddest experiences was...
The happiest day of my life was...
In springtime I feel...
When I see a newborn baby I feel...
When I see an old person I think about...
The person I miss the most is ... because...
When I was young my worst fear was...
I believe (or don't believe) that I am lovable because...
When I can't sleep in the dark of night my thoughts turn to...
I pretend that I like...
If I could change my life I would do...
I hope that on my deathbed I don't regret...

Part II

After you have completed your inventory take some time to go back to each line item and recall a person or event that may have influenced your perception of yourself and your accomplishments or failures with regard to that issue or item. Now that time has intervened, some space exists between your perceptions of yourself and those implied by others. This may allow you to re-evaluate their opinions, and perhaps to unearth their hidden agendas around you, which might have been previously missed. This investigation may be emotionally challenging, but this exercise will assist you in becoming more in touch with yourself and your feelings.

Being Okay With Strengths and Weaknesses

If you cry openly at sad movies, so be it; if you laugh a little too loudly, or snort like a pig when you really let loose, then that's okay. If you have a temper, or punish people with silence, if you have a jealous streak or secretly wish people unhappiness, fess up, at least to yourself. Then decide which of these things will prevent you from becoming an effective step-parent, keeping in mind that step-parenting isn't just about taking care of someone else's child. Step-parenting is about really allowing yourself to love a human being who wasn't born from your body, but whose entire life can be impacted by you just the same.

Conversely, if you are not certain about your character attributes and flaws, you may find yourself wallowing in self-pity or seething in anger every time something doesn't go your way; if this is the case we suggest you prepare yourself for the inevitable because there will be plenty of times that will be the case. However, if you can rise above the fray, secure in your position, comfortable in your own skin, with a strong sense of who you are and where you are going, even your staunchest dissenters will soften to your honesty. In the business of step-parenting, you are an ambassador of sorts, bridging together splintered families, soothing children who have been wounded on the divorce battlefields, blending your new family and your old family with sensitivity and humor, warmth and compassion, patience and love.

Rebecca's Story

Rebecca was tearful throughout most of her first meeting with us; she had difficulty expressing her feelings other than to indicate that she felt excluded within her blended family. When we asked her to give examples to illuminate these feelings of exclusion, she seemed embarrassed, as if her examples would seem frivolous when they were put into words. Clearly she had difficulty communicating her feelings. At the end of her first session we invited her to go home and work with the questions in the Personal Inventory. Over the next week she begin jotting down some specific examples of situations that have caused her much emotional pain.

As we anticipated, Rebecca's journaling in the privacy of her home allowed her to be less inhibited. The following week, when she produced her journal, it was evident that the common denominator of every situation was her insecurity about her new role as a step-parent, defined by her spouse's mother (Helen) who happened to live on the same block. At first it appeared to Rebecca that she was accepted by Helen, especially since Helen offered her assistance even when Rebecca hadn't asked for it; she always managed to drop by the house with the children's favorite cookies or a casserole just as the children stepped off the school bus. But Rebecca soon noticed her feelings of insecurity intensified when she could never seem to come up with the "right" directives to her step-children. If Rebecca told them they could go out to play, Helen suggested they finish their homework first; if Rebecca offered them one of Helen's home-made cookies, Helen reminded Rebecca that the cookies were for dessert only after the children cleaned their dinner plates. At first Rebecca was grateful for these helpful parenting hints, but over time she found that she couldn't make any decisions without Helen stepping in with the last word.

Rebecca was grateful for her mother-in-law's "mentoring" but she was becoming increasingly unhappy that none of her own choices seemed to be correct. By the end of Rebecca's second session in our office it was obvious that without a clear sense of herself, her self-esteem would continue to spiral downward at the hands of her meddling, albeit helpful, mother-in-law. We crafted a treatment plan carefully and cautiously so that Rebecca's anticipated self worth did not become a threat to her step-children's grandmother, which would place her husband in the center of what might become a family dispute.

Rebecca did her homework! Before long she began embracing her strengths and forgiving herself for past mistakes. She learned that her inexperience with children did not overshadow the valuable attributes she brought to the table. In three weeks Rebecca was ready to sit down with her mother-in-law on a more level playing field. She explained that she did not blame her mother-in-law for stepping in, but that her insecurities were based upon fear and uncertainty. She explained that she was an observant and vigilant individual who would, to the best of her ability, not allow any harm to come to the children in her charge. When Rebecca asserted herself and her new-found confidence in the meeting, her mother-in-law admitted that she had reservations about Rebecca's commitment to the children based upon her lack of parenting experience. By clearing up prior unspoken doubts, the two women worked out a schedule whereby Rebecca would take more charge of her step-children, and her mother-in-law would support her decisions openly.

Two months after the "meeting" Rebecca came in to happily report that she and her mother-in-law found a nice balance of mutual friendship based solely upon getting to know each other. Rebecca welcomes her mother-in-law's short, bi-weekly visits with the kids, and has found herself at the center of praise for her quickly learned parenting skills.

No One Has All the Answers

Rebecca's story is an example of the importance of having a more complete sense of yourself. Without this, you may be easily swayed by the opinions of others based upon nothing more than your lack of confidence. In Rebecca's case, once she recognized that no one parent has all of the answers, and that no one method of parenting is better or worse than the other—as long as the method involves love, boundaries, praise and consequences within reason of a child's level of emotional and physical maturity—she moved forward with eager enthusiasm and enjoyment in her role as a step-parent. More importantly, she was viewed by the outside world as an individual who made good decisions and with whom the children could be trusted.

❖

If you are unsure of who you are (and who isn't to some degree), you need to really work on asking yourself important questions that can help you to gain insight. If people perceive you in a manner that is unfair and inaccurate—a common scenario—take a step back from this identification. You do not have to behave according to their expectations. What would it mean to be true to yours?

Children are great judges of character; they can spot an imposter from a mile away, and worse, have no qualms about exposing you. They are also forgiving. If they know you are doing the best you can, that you may make some mistakes along the way, but that you always have their best interest at heart, they will support, defend, and love you.

STRATEGY #2
Examine Your Expectations

Mary was both thrilled and frightened. Bob had decided it was time to bring his three children (ages five, seven and ten) to meet her. He had obviously committed to this next step in their growing relationship, but what if they didn't like her?

Bob believed the children would be on their best behavior if they met at Mary's house. She was not so sure. She didn't have much experience with children, other than a few babysitting jobs back in high school, but the one thing she knew was that children and toys were a match.

The day before the scheduled meeting Mary tore the house apart, vacuuming the carpet and cleaning bathrooms. She then spent the afternoon at the local toy store, filling a shopping cart with colorful plastic toys and coloring books. The finishing touches kept her busy well into the night, with every square inch of pantry and refrigerator loaded with healthy snacks; she even snuck in some junk food and ice cream as an insurance policy!

By the time Bob and the kids arrived the next day Mary was a frazzled mess; she hadn't slept well and she looked it. Her home was so perfectly put together that even she felt uncomfortable in her own surroundings. Within minutes after she had distributed toys, the two younger children began fighting over who was going to play with what; while the older child seemed aloof and indifferent, wanting nothing to do with "baby" toys and coloring books. Mary then offered a newly-released children's video, which she had rented. No sooner had she turned it on than the children notified her that they had viewed it the night before at their mother's house, with the ten-year-old emphasizing the word "mother."

The children refused lunch, but were intrigued by the cake and ice cream, leaving sticky fingerprints along the chair cushions and table. They had little interest in Mary and even less interest in showing gratitude for the effort she had made. Mary was not only disappointed but angry—first at what she perceived to be thoughtless and unappreciative children, but later at Bob who didn't seem to be aware of her feelings and his rude children. Mary felt Bob should have done more to make the children "like" her, and by the time the couple came to couple's therapy it was clear that Bob and Mary were at odds.

Unrealistic Expectations

As in so many areas of the step-parenting challenge, both adults in the story above were guilty of unrealistic expectations. In retrospect, Mary realized that regardless of the scenario she created in her mind, children were just that ... *children*. Their behavior, while agreeably in need of some prior etiquette-teaching, was also not unlike the unpredictable behavior of their age groups, especially as their father was expecting them to "welcome" another woman who was not their mother. Bob should have explained to the children, prior to the meeting, that although they may not know his "friend," he expected them to be courteous and gracious. When they were not, he might have given them a private reminder by taking them aside during the visit.

In his defense, Bob admitted that he hadn't had much training in child-rearing, having left most of the "hands on" application of manners and rules to his former wife. To her defense, Mary admitted that she hadn't had much patience after putting herself through an exhausting attempt at "buying" the children's affection. Both had viable explanations, but none was acceptable as a reasonable response for "getting off the hook." Bob should have been more supportive of Mary's feelings, taking into consideration her lack of experience with children's normal self-centeredness. Mary might have spent more time trying to find some common ground with the children's interests, rather than distracting them with material objects and food lures.

After their initial visit to our office, Mary and Bob and the children, with our encouragement and their own more realistic evaluation of everyone's expectations, held their second meeting at a neutral site. Mary was much more relaxed. She stood on the sidelines as she observed Bob and his children, and before long they were asking her advice and begging to sit next to her at lunch. It didn't take long for Mary and Bob to understand that children ask only that the adults in their lives genuinely want to be with them in a lighthearted manner without the expectations which almost always ruin any scenario.

An Expectation Inventory

Sometimes, when expectations are unrealistic, they place goals so far out of reach that working toward attaining those goals feels hopeless. Before you examine just how realistic your expectations are, we invite you to take our Expectation Inventory assessment. As always, these statement fragments are simply guidelines; please add as many extra statements as you can think of in your quest to examine your expectations, and feel free to discard any of ours that do not pertain to you. It is always best to try to complete this assignment within a few days, so that your frame of mind is consistent, and your focus remains clear.

You may be surprised at how close you are to attaining your expectations. Once they are actually spelled out in black and white, you may find that you can quickly rework those that you first identified as "unrealistic."

There will not be enough room on the page to fill in all your thoughts, so please add these items to your journal or notebook where you worked with the "Self-Inventory" from Chapter 1.

While you are assessing your expectations, please keep three questions in mind:

1. What am I expecting here?
2. Who is ultimately responsible for this?
3. How would I like to be or to act in this situation? Good luck!
4. When I attempt something I am apt to…
5. When I feel defeated I will most likely…
6. If I am in a new area of learning I…
7. If I do not succeed at first try I…
8. If I believe that other people will be scrutinizing my work I…
9. If I am not the "best" at something, or the "quickest" at something, I…
10. I meet challenges…
11. I feel defeated when…
12. If the task is too difficult I am likely to…
13. I will ask for help if…
14. I am most likely to be my own worst critic because…

This Expectation Inventory will help you to recognize areas of strength in your new role as step-parent, as well as those tendencies that may ultimately sabotage your goals. For example, if you are an individual who expects to master a new task immediately, your ability to weather the ups and downs of any parenting situation will be more challenged. Or, if you feel comfortable asking for assistance, you will probably feel good about your accomplishments even though you didn't meet your goal independently.

How you handle your own expectations is an indicator of how your emotions might interfere with your goals. If your Expectation Inventory reveals areas of unrealistic demands (on yourself or others) give yourself permission to seek assistance and make mistakes. Recognize that every moment offers a new learning experience, and one that can propel you toward your goal.

R-H-D-A

When it comes to your expectations of others, try this helpful tip:

RECOGNIZE those priorities that you believe should be addressed or modified by you or both you and your partner. Remember that not all issues can be "fixed" but certainly they can be made more acceptable and positive.

HONOR your vows to each other and yourself; you are part of a parenting team, and as such, must remember to display respect and open communication, as well as to be receptive to commentary.

DE-FUSE when you find yourself approaching a meltdown. Remove yourself from the situation, take some deep breaths, give any situation that doesn't require immediate action a day or two to gain perspective, and then revisit those issues that still require resolution.

ACCEPT. Not every situation can be re-arranged to your liking. Such is life! Be fair with yourself, your spouse, and your step-children when you make requests or evaluate situations. Those things that cannot be changed, can often be viewed from a different vantage point or with a more accepting eye. Keep your options open.

No individual feels good about themselves all the time. No one person always knows what to do or how to act in every situation. To conquer fears of the unknown, there must be some stumbling, falling and getting back up. Don't be so hard on yourself, you are only human. Timing (and patience) is everything!

Now that you have a better understanding of your own unique self-expectations, the adjustments you might decide to make in certain areas will pave the way for a stronger and healthier relationship as a spouse and step-parent. In this chapter you will have an opportunity to apply what you've learned as we consider the following issues: initial meetings; serious plans— like moving and weddings; discipline and boundary setting; relating to the former spouse; sharing memories, and welcoming extended family members.

Meeting Your New Step-Children

Some of you may have already known your step-children in another capacity before you married their biologic parent. You may have been their neighbor, their school teacher, or have children who attend the same schools as your step-children, but for the most part, many of you will be meeting your step-children for the first time. This meeting can have lasting impact upon your relationship with them, so for those of you anticipating this step, it should be well thought out. What are you expecting? This is a good time to recall your expectation strategies, particularly those that may be unreasonable.

In retrospect, many step-parents who were interviewed about their initial contact with their soon-to-be step-children agreed that their fear of not being accepted was overwhelming. They recounted their feelings of helplessness and trepidation. While the outcome is unpredictable, the examination of expectations is a help to everyone concerned. Often these feelings have roots in other events that mimic the same feelings of treading on uncertain ground.

Meeting your step-children for the first time is not unlike being interviewed for employment. Even if you excel in your area of expertise, there is no guarantee of a successful outcome. You are not always judged on accomplishments, but rather on any random, non-specific factor, such as physical attributes, mannerisms or ethnicity. In the case of step-parents, you will be judged, often unfairly, by children based upon their own unresolved emotions or whimsical expectations. Their conclusions may very well be impulsive, erratic, biased and subject to change on a moment to moment basis. However, these emotions will form conclusions that will weigh heavily in the overall dynamics of the family unit.

We point this out not to discourage you but to remind you of the value of being prepared. Often, when impulses want immediate gratification, it is necessary to remember that "slow and steady wins the race." Although it is difficult to be openly disregarded, it is best not to take to heart the sullen, withdrawn, defiant, moody or indifferent behaviors of children. They have their own expectations, and an agenda to which you are not privy. These kids may only be three or four years of age, however, they should not be underestimated. They have the ability to make your life miserable if they are so inclined. Teenagers are especially prone to stir the pot of emotions, practicing manipulations for their own gain.

Expecting to Like Your Step-Children

Nearly the entire step-parenting population wants to like their step-children, but unfortunately sometimes they don't seem like a good match. The problems may lie with your step-kids being unruly, unappreciative or just plain spoiled, or the problems may lie with you being ill-equipped to deal with the daily trials of someone else's children. Either way, the conflicts that arise from these negative feelings almost always trickle down to your marital relationship, impacting it negatively.

We know the trauma that divorced children have experienced, and we understand the shortcomings and unrealistic expectations your spouse may have had in imagining that the children would instantly "click" with you, but what about opening up *your* emotional suitcases to see what is hidden inside with regard to caring for children.

Aside from your own childhood experiences and your painful adult experiences, like failed former marriages and the fallout from divorce, there are things you may not know about yourself until you have to confront them. That you fell in love with your partner has little bearing on how you feel about your step-children. Truth be told, not everyone *likes* children. Those of you who like them may not *understand* them, and those of you who both like and understand children, in general, may not specifically like *your* step-children. As embarrassing as this might be to admit, some of you actually do not like your step-children.

Loving Equally? — Biologic Children "Versus" Step-Children

Before you jump to conclusions about feeling as though your personality is not a good match with your step-children, or that you are not equipped to deal with someone else's children, there are other related issues and expectations to be examined. Perhaps it isn't so much that you dislike your step-children as it is that you are comparing your feelings for your biologic children to your step-kid. This is a common mistake and can be corrected.

Few step-parents can honestly say that they share equally the love of their children and step-children. But, these same step-parents may easily forget that, when parenting their biologic children, there were stages the children went through that made them quite unlikeable. The "terrible twos" come to mind, as well as prepubescent and teenage rebellious years, when young people become notoriously self-centered and impossibly distant from all but their circle of friends. Suzanne's story reflects the challenges of one stage of child development.

It is rarely possible to love your step-children with the same degree of intensity and maternal or paternal instinct as you do your biologic children. Some of you may disagree with this concept but we hold fast to our opinion based on years of experiences with hundreds of blended families. Regardless of how much you might wish things differently, you are bound by genetics and bonding in infancy. You will not love your step-children *in the same way* as you love your biologic children. Even biologic children who have left the nest, or with whom you have cut ties, are still bound to you by invisible strings. Biologic parents actually feel the pain of their child's injury, and heartache when their child is emotionally distraught. This same physical reaction may not occur to the same degree with your step-children. This is not to imply that as a step-parent you will not feel the heartache of disappointment or the distress when your step-children experience physical pain, but the intensities are probably going to be different. This is not something your step-children should know, but something that you must be aware of because your reaction is normal.

You may love your step-children, evaluate their behavior objectively, and even wish your biologic children behaved more like your step-children, but you will never be able to replicate the love you bear for the children of your body.

This is such an important concept, with many implications. It explains why you might feel you are being disloyal to your biologic children if you love your step-children. It explains why, to avoid this perception of disloyalty, you may distance yourself, unconsciously, from your step-children. It explains why you feel pushed to defend your biologic child against your step-child in a verbal or physical altercation. This knowledge is meant to relieve you of any unnecessary guilt. Even though as an adult you are responsible to act appropriately, your feeling-responses are normal!

Suzanne's Story

Suzanne couldn't have chosen a worse time to become a step-mother. Her step-twins were two years old and their behavior re-defined the description of the "terrible twos." They crumbled into temper tantrums over the least little things, and reacted to nearly everything in a negative manner. Jim, Suzanne's husband of only two months, was not particularly flustered by their antics, but he was insulated to the chaos because of his large family of origin. Suzanne, on the other hand, was an only child and lived in an orderly and quiet household. She was also new to parenting, having no biologic children of her own.

Jim came home from work most nights only to find his wife in tears. His remedy of becoming stricter with the twins only seemed to backfire, and when he came into our office he was at a complete loss as to how to proceed. Suzanne's ultimatum had been issued: Either he had to "make" his children behave or he needed to limit the amount of time the children were allowed to "visit" their home.

With a lack of parenting experience comes little under-standing of children's developmental milestones. Suzanne certainly lacked the experience, but she more than made up for this limitation by her motivation to learn as much as she could as fast as she could. With therapy she learned to redirect her frustrations into creative methods of distracting her step-children from their own negativity, turning temper tantrums into fun adventures.

After a couple months of family therapy Suzanne was very adept at managing both their outbursts and their achievements, boosting her confidence as she counted the days until they turned three. She realized that there would be other developmental challenges, but this time she would be prepared.

Ellen's Story

Ellen strove to be the best step-parent she could be. She read all the books written on the subject, met with step-parenting groups, and tried to learn everything about the two children she was about to raise. But, one thing she was unable to come to terms with was her bias toward her biologic children. She kept it in check, of course, and promised herself that she would be completely fair and equal to all of the children in her blended family, but during day-to-day events, she wanted to "rescue" her biologic children from the mean things or actions her step-children delivered.

When she did defend her biologic children, her step-children called her prejudiced; when she attempted to defend her step-children, her biologic children felt betrayed. Ellen felt completely inadequate and began basing her decisions about boundaries, and her discipline with the children on nothing more than trying to keep everyone happy. Thus, in a self-fulfilling prophecy, she started to become inadequate. By the time she came into therapy, she was waking in the middle of the night with panic-anxiety attacks.

Over the next several months we assisted Ellen with creating a Behavior-Consequence chart (see Strategy #3) so that all the children would be treated in the same manner. Now it was *they* who would make a choice to behave properly or suffer a consequence.

One of the approaches that Ellen found to be most helpful was to schedule time alone with her biologic children while her step-children were visiting with their biologic mother. This strengthened her bond with her kids without her step-children feeling left out. However, we warned her that any major activities, such as a trip to Disney World or a ski vacation, should be shared equally, lest there be negative feelings—of rejection—among any of the group. This approach seemed to ease her burden. It wasn't long before the children realized that their manipulations, which had previously pulled her from one side to the other, were no longer successful.

Separating the Behavior from the Child

Often it is not your step-children that you do not like, but rather their behavior. Children are by definition self-centered, self-absorbed little people who have no regard for anyone else's time, money or feelings. Their insatiable needs propel them to badger, beg, plead or manipulate almost every situation for their own gain, without remorse or conscience. If these manipulations work, even inconsistently, the fire is fanned for more of the same.

Behavior can be modified! And we will deal at length with that subject in Strategy #3, where we explain the Family Hierarchy Ladder and the use of Behavior-Consequence chart.

Nevertheless, if you honestly believe that there is something about your step-children that makes *them* unlovable, you have only two options: The first is to fake it. That option will not last very long, not to mention that it incorporates lying, which, as you already know, is one of our pet peeves. The second option is to tell your spouse the truth and enter into family therapy or parenting classes to see if the situation can be identified properly and rectified. The therapist can assist you in examining your feelings, recognizing those that may be contaminated with the unresolved stuff in your emotional suitcase. If they are, then at least you will know that your luggage was already weighed down before you even met your step-children.

Children's Expectations

Face it, your new step-children feel threatened by you, or at least by the newness of the situation. Children will always wish for what *was*, and will use the tool of bargaining to try to get it. In other words, children will promise their parents that they will feed their pets, clean their room, take out the garbage, and overall be "perfect" if only their parent will reconsider choosing *you* over the other biologic parent. Personalizing their behavior and their attempts to "territorialize" their parent will only drive a wedge between you and them, and between you and your new partner. Instead, recognize their expectations, honor them, and accept that you present a very real threat to them, and that they are using their behaviors as the only weapons they possess to protect their home. These skilled manipulators have only one focus. In order to understand just how you might be perceived as the "enemy," consider this fundamental premise: most if not all children of divorce wish their parents back together. That wish cannot be fulfilled if you interrupt their plans by "stealing" the parent. You have spoiled everything; you have not only managed to steal one parent, you have wreaked havoc with the other. At least that is the way many of them will view you initially. So, when their parent announces plans to remarry, all their hopes and plans come crashing down around them.

The other biologic parent, although not physically present, might as well be for the acute awareness that parent holds in the minds of the children. These children may be mentally at battle with feelings of disloyalty and betrayal. Above all else, children do not want to inflict pain on the other parent, and many of them believe that if they *like* you, they have crossed the loyalty line and hurt their parent. This confusion not only comes from immature thinking, but often is promoted and fostered by the other parent in question. Children are very black and white in their thinking. They don't understand that by accepting you they have not discarded their biologic parent. Shifting loyalties causes disruption in their sleep and confusion in their waking hours. If the parents of these children have been unable to find it in their hearts to put the interest of their children foremost, you will not only find yourself in an unfair quandary, you may very well have to assist these adults to mend fences.

Ryan's Story

Ryan and his brother Ned remember meeting Coach Derrick for the first time while they were playing pee-wee football; they were ten and eleven years old. They liked Coach Derrick and especially loved it when their mother came to their games and stayed afterward talking to the other moms and the coach. Their father rarely made it to the games because of his late work schedule.

Five years later, when their parents announced they were getting a divorce, the boys were devastated. Their sadness grew worse when, six months after their father moved out of the house, their mother began dating Coach Derrick. Although in reality there had been no infidelity, it appeared to the boys and their friends that something must have been "going on." When their mother asked where they had gotten such an idea, the boys unanimously said, "Dad told us." Although the boys wanted to believe their mother, they hated it when Coach Derrick looked at her "that way." It took an unusually long time for them to trust Derrick because of the emotional contamination of their father's opinion.

Depending on their ages, children will display their expectations, anxieties and insecurities about your inclusion in the family by various forms of behavior. Young children may experience temper tantrums, nightmares, bedwetting and clinginess to their parent. Older children may become withdrawn and sullen, or openly defiant and rebellious; this behavior is especially true in children who have reached the stage of "perceived independence." They are less than thrilled at the prospect of yet another "authority figure" squeezing their way into what they view as an already crowded circle of policing adults. Regardless of your understated presence, children are all too aware that, should you decide to remain in the family even after they have pulled out every trump card they can think of to force you out, you will be another set of eyes and ears in their lives.

Without exception, your step-children are the victims of their parent's divorce or death. Every one of them has suffered a great emotional blow, and each of them has relied upon some type of coping mechanism to survive emotionally. It is easy to personalize rejection by labeling your step-children as rude or ill-mannered, but beneath the indifferent or rebellious exterior is a lost child who stood by powerless as their lives were dismantled: homes were sold, furniture was divided, residences were downsized, neighborhoods vanished. Lifelong friends were left behind and pets were given away. These children didn't magically wake up to a brand new day; they worked at carving out new lives, new schools and new friends. They learned to live out of suitcases as they moved from one parent's house to the other for their "visitation." Finally, life became a little more normal. There was less fighting and more smiling. Their little faces reflected times of innocence once more. That is, until *you* came along.

From their perspective, they owe you nothing. You are neither their relative nor their friend. To the contrary, you are the troublemaker who showed up to ruin everything. This is the worst of it for you; this is the time in which you will be judged unfairly and unmercifully. Regardless of how hard you try, you will not win their affection until *they* are ready, and for each child that amount of time varies.

Expectations for Good

The one thing to know is this: Your step-children will eventually learn to love you, not because they must, but because they so much want to believe in family unity, in civilized adults, in unbroken promises and in love. Children are nothing if not resilient. They want to believe you when you say you will never leave them. They crave stability.

To answer the question, "How does any new step-parent have a chance?" our advice is basic common knowledge: all you have to do is be yourself. Children despise imposters, even when they are on the receiving end of an overly generous adult. Food and gifts do not necessarily give you a free pass into the hearts of children. You may think of yourself as the greatest actor in the world, but you will not deceive a child.

When you meet soon-to-be step-children, don't appear nicer than you actually are, or you will outshine your own personality. If you tend to be introverted, then by all means be quiet; if you tend to be extroverted, be prepared to carry your bubbly personality forth throughout the rest of your entire relationship with your step-children or be later thought of as a fake. Our advice is this: When attempting to build a trusting relationship, don't begin that relationship with a lie.

Be yourself! If you master this, your meetings have a much better chance of being positive and fruitful ... *Well, not always* (as the case of Raymond and Linda that follows will show). The splintering of the previous family unit is a determining factor in how the new step-parent will be received. Regardless of how "real" you are, it would be unrealistic to expect an overnight transformation in your children. The manner in which the divorce was handled long before you came on the scene has great influence on the degree to which you will or will not be welcomed.

Nonetheless, one part within your step-children's minds and hearts will trust you to repair their lopsided view of love and fidelity; they need you to be the real deal. If you remember that they are fragile and vulnerable, pace yourself, wait it out patiently, and offer a hand when they reach for it, they will invest themselves in you to an unbelievable degree. You had nothing to do with their divorce trauma, but you have everything to do with their recovery. Raymond's story illustrates how failure to appreciate children's expectations and the pain they suffer from divorce can be devastating to everyone.

Raymond's Story

Raymond, a divorced father, made an appointment for his three children—ages twelve, fourteen and fifteen—because of their purposeful insolence to his fiancée, Linda. From the moment the children learned that what they presumed was casual dating had turned into a marriage proposal they were angry and outwardly rebellious. Their words were negative and hurtful, said impulsively and with anger to their soon-to-be step-mother, prompting Raymond to respond to them in kind. By the time they came into the therapy office, there was tension, anger and hurt feelings all around.

The three children tearfully recounted the pain they felt during the divorce process, and the anguish they especially felt for their mother, Shirley, who was nearly paralyzed in grief. Although they resided with their mother, for the most part, they worried about how she would pay for their modest apartment, since their father had remained in the marital home. Still, Raymond retained their bedrooms just as they had always been, encouraging them to spend as much time with him as they liked.

Although the children recalled years of angry accusations between their parents, they still wanted their parents to get back together. Even when the divorce was final, the children did not give up. Rather, they spent an exorbitant amount of energy plotting to rekindle their parents' romance. Whenever they overheard Mom and Dad apparently getting along on the telephone, their expectations were positive, certain that any semblance of civility was another building block in restructuring their relationship. Then, their father introduced them to Linda, dashing their plans and dreams. Before long, as Raymond and Linda were talking of marriage, the children believed that their mother would be unable to cope with their dad's remarriage.

After spending several therapy sessions with the children individually, we called in both biologic parents, Raymond and Shirley. We explained that their children's unrealistic expectations about a renewed relationship was now dashed because of the "interference" of another woman. The biologic parents began to understand that the children would not accept Linda without their support. They recognized the need to communicate to the children that, regardless of *who* might enter into the scenario, or even if there never was the addition of another individual, their marriage was over! Because of the love they had for their children, Raymond and Shirley took the mature path. In their presence, Raymond promised the children he would always "take care of" Shirley by including her in any family event hosted at his home. Shirley agreed to do the same, this time with a conviction in her voice that she would be strong enough to move forward. At the same time, Shirley went beyond what was asked of her. She told the children that she had spoken to Linda on the telephone, and she would be fully supportive of her marriage to Raymond provided she was a good step-mother to the children. "All I ever wanted was for you kids to be happy. If she can love you half as much as I do, I think we'll all be okay."

Everyone Expects Honesty ... Including the Children!

Honesty About Dating

Once major introductions have melted into courtship, the manner in which this courtship is carried out is directly linked to your acceptance in the family. At its inception, dating should be open; children have little patience for discovering that while Dad said he had a late night meeting he in fact was on a date. Whether children express the desire for their parent to date, or hold fast to the notion that their parents may some day rekindle their relationship if dating is somehow stopped, approaching the issue with the truth is always the best solution. Why? Again, when it comes to children, honesty beats out deception every time.

As well, if you haven't been upfront with other family members, like grandparents, aunts, or uncles, it places these others at an unfair disadvantage when your children become aware of the deception, as if these adults may have acted in collusion. If you do confide in others, they also become accessories to your deception, if only by default.

If you decide to date, your children may be disappointed, but it will also help them to appreciate that their biologic parents are less likely to reconnect. Also, as soon as you become aware that a dating situation is leading to something more permanent, it should really become a "family affair."

Honesty In Living Arrangements

Following courtship, the next level of commitment either becomes marriage or cohabitation. We do not endorse living together before marriage when there are children involved for reasons that involve morality and role-modeling. Even in this permissive twenty-first century, where cohabitation is more the rule than the exception, you are cheapening yourself in the eyes of the children; these are their sentiments not ours, as we've heard repeatedly in our therapy practice. They are embarrassed for themselves and they are embarrassed in front of their friends. Even if your marriage is just months away, if at all possible, try to make other living arrangements.

Many of you will disagree with this, citing several reasons to support financial and geographic convenience as important factors to be considered. We have especially noticed that adults love to defend the importance of children observing closeness and affection that was so often missing in their family of origin. This is a convenient argument but it isn't strong enough to trump children's feelings; they are "creeped out" by witnessing almost any form of intimacy, and they've told us so!

Also, nothing sends the other biologic parent into a spin faster than finding out that the children's biologic parent and not-yet step-parent have decided to "shack- up" together. This is not college, where anything goes; this is real adult life with the psyches of real step-children. Practicing behaviors that most others will label as "immoral" does no one any good, and certainly not the person who you are going to need on your side—the other biologic parent. If you and your step-kids want to start out on the right foot, spend the night with your new partner when the step-children are not there, and at no other time. We stand firm on that advice. The messages that are given to children by role-modeling should not be blurred. We know you want to give the right message, but that message has to be clear enough to be interpreted accurately by your children. Regardless of the societal new-age belief that life is just one great big hedonistic free-for-all, children have not changed. They need role modeling, values and standards by which to live. They know it, and their other biologic parent knows it, which is why you can dodge a whole lot of bullets by simply getting married instead of dragging out a long engagement.

If you feel you just can't live apart from your fiancé, then get married. It's just that simple. If you are so much in love that you refuse to live separately, then we believe you are in love enough to support the institution of marriage for the sake of your step-children.

That goes for family vacations prior to marriage as well; if you are planning to take the children on overnight excursions, plan on getting separate rooms. You can take them to Disney World or you can even take them to the moon and back, provided the accommodations do not include the two of you cavorting in the same bed. Even a picture with Mickey Mouse cannot wipe away the mental image of impropriety.

Before marriage the rule of thumb is this: keep it buttoned, zipped, closed and private.

Honesty in Communication

About The Wedding
Immediately after the two of you decide to marry, we suggest that all the children be told either simultaneously or as soon as possible. Whether the children are reluctant, angry, disappointed, happy or indifferent, withholding wedding information isn't going to change the real fact that there will be a wedding. If you are on good terms with your former spouses, this is the time to call them directly and tell them the news, not because they will necessarily be thrilled to hear it, but because they need to know factual information. This takes away any possibility of your step-children being placed in a position of carrying the burden of what they believe may be devastating news. If you and your former spouse are not on good enough terms for you to notify him or her directly, please tell your children that this news is not a secret, and that they have your permission to share it with their other biologic parent.

About Arrangements in General
We are advocates of adults acting maturely where children are concerned. We hope that all the adults in question have worked out their differences enough that they can now spend time alleviating any fears the children may have regarding the changes that are about to occur, and about how those changes will impact their lives.

If your former spouse has not met your intended bride or groom, depending on your individual situation find a method of introduction. For instance, if you are on very good terms, plan a small dinner party where the children can view first-hand their parents welcoming in the newest members of the soon-to-be blended families, including the children of both parties. If not, at least make a call and introduce them by telephone. Let's see how Jack decided to handle this dilemma.

Jack's Story

Jack had maintained a good relationship with his former spouse in the two years following their divorce, but he still felt uneasy as he grappled with announcing his plans to remarry. It wasn't so much that his former wife Anita was still in love with him, but rather that he didn't want her to feel betrayed if he gloated over his happiness with another woman. When he came into the therapy office he seemed like a man who couldn't win no matter how he tried to think of every angle. His biggest wish would be to just let his former wife hear the news from his children, so that he didn't have to face hurting her. He assured us he wouldn't be such a coward if only she had moved on with her personal life. But Anita hadn't. Instead, she sat at home without dates month after month.

With our encouragement Jack saw that it was unfair to assume that he could use his children as the bearers of this news. He was able to appreciate that they were ill-equipped to deal with any negative emotions that Anita might unload. Kindness dictated that everyone be as sensitive as possible, but Jack agreed that this included being honest and forthright with information that would certainly reach Anita through the grapevine if he did not take responsibility for communicating it himself. He acknowledged that receiving news indirectly from unknown sources would be both devastating and humiliating. Surely that would not be advantageous if he hoped to support any sort of relationship between himself and Anita, and between Anita and his new wife.

For the better part of one week Jack rehearsed a speech that he had written in the event he was at a loss for words, but there was no need. When Anita met Jack in our office, she sat quietly, almost willing him confidence. It was clear that although their marriage didn't work, they still had a deep connection and open communication. Anita shed a few tears, but had no bitterness for her former husband. All that she asked was that his intended wife be a good step-mother to their children. When he asked if she would like to meet her, Anita readily agreed. We gave Jack the option of having the two women meet in our therapy office if his anxieties were too great. Prior to that meeting, however, he left a message on our answering machine saying that all had gone well.

Expectations and Intimacy

We understand that new love is hypnotic; that often you can't eat or sleep or concentrate on anything else but the person you adore. It is almost as if the two of you are united by electricity, and without thinking you will want to be as physically close to your love as possible. However, here is a sobering word of caution: If your step-children are old enough to know about the birds and bees, they have already figured out that the two of you are more than "friends." *They know it, but they don't want to dwell on it.* To process this type of information puts their little minds on overload, and there is no need to belabor the point by putting on a display of physical affection. They get it—you have intimacy!

During your courtship, therefore, be mindful of children's expectations around your expressions of intimacy with your new partner. When the children (biologic or step-children) are present, avoid any sexual innuendos and inferences towards your adult love-interest. Keep this play for later, in private moments, rather than expressing it in public forums. Nothing is more repulsive for a child than to think of their parents in any way other than just being ... well ... their *parents*! The idea that their parent and soon-to be step-parent share intimacy literally causes them to cringe. Specifically, you should not be a party to anything more than casual hand-holding or a friendly peck on the cheek while in the presence of the children during the courtship phase, and for a longer period with many children. Anything more than this is embarrassing and unacceptable from their perspective, and seconded by us.

We have lost count of the number of step-children who have told us how disgusted and disappointed they feel when they witness their biologic parent in an intimate setting with their step-parent. Most of them never witnessed this type of intimacy between their biologic parents, since the thrill likely had worn off before their birth, or certainly during the months or years preceding the divorce.

Your children have a childhood to concentrate on, the focus of which becomes clouded when sexual inferences filter in. As adults, you should have mastered impulse control. If you truly can't keep your hands off each other, do everyone a favor by securing a babysitter and a hotel room. Please, enjoy your intimacy, be thrilled by it, indulge yourselves in privacy, but in public, keep it rated PG.

Sophie and Ned's Story

One of the few moments when the Stafford children could break away from their busy schedules was for Thursday movie night. After their parents' divorce it was decided that the kids would spend every Thursday night with their dad lying around the living room in their pajamas, eating popcorn and watching a movie. Nothing interfered with movie night, not even Ned's work schedule. But when Ned introduced Sophie to the children, everything was about to change.

Noticeably the children were uncomfortable spending time in their pajamas in front of someone outside the family, so it was decided that they would all dress for movies, which changed the entire atmosphere of the event. Then the pillow fights stopped, and finally the usual rib-jabbing and inside jokes gave way to silence and seats on the couch. Sophie and their father threw a blanket on the empty space on the floor, and week by week they'd lie there uninterested in the movie, but certainly interested in each other. One especially chilly Thursday night they added a blanket over them, and beneath the fabric it was clear that their hands were not kept to themselves.

The following week, and the week after that, the children came up with excuses as to why they could not attend movie night. Ned was upset and disappointed, but had no idea that it was he who had sabotaged his own event. In therapy, when the children finally let loose, they told him in no uncertain terms that he was disgusting and they didn't expect their father to "act like that."

Ned spoke with Sophie about movie night and asked her to bow out; she refused. Though it was difficult, he made the right choice and told Sophie he could no longer date her if she was not able to respect the children's wishes.

Movie nights are back on track now, and regardless of who might come into the picture, Ned has learned his lesson about the sanctity of this ritual.

Most children love physical affection from their parents. Some, depending on their ages, will warm up fairly quickly to physical forms of expression from a step-parent, while others shy away. It is difficult to "time" when physical affection is appropriate, but a general rule is that children are very clever clue providers. In other words, if your step-child comes up to give you a hug, or takes your hand on a walk, they are ready for a return of physical affection.

If, as a step-parent, you are a natural "touchy-feely" individual, you may find yourself having to tone down your personality. For others, who may feel uncomfortable displaying physical affection, we recommend that if you are invited to do so by your step-children, you should take the risk! While such expressions may feel awkward at first, you will be pleasantly surprised how quickly they become second-nature!

STRATEGY #3
Use the Hierarchy Ladder
A Short Course in Family Dynamics

The Family Hierarchy is one of our favorite topics. We discuss its use in every parenting book we write. Without this vital information, and without you and your partner mutually agreeing about it, there is little to sustain any order in your household.

The Family Hierarchy, depicted as a ladder, is a blueprint that clearly delineates boundaries, and illustrates how one person in the family interacts with another. If boundaries are not well defined, family members are prone to "flip-flop" from one position to another—from assuming authority that isn't theirs, to relinquishing responsibility that *is*—with ensuing chaos and turmoil. This chaos is eliminated in using the Family Hierarchy Ladder. Its premise is that your family is not a democracy. Therefore, decision-making in your family will not be a democratic process.

If you feel stunned by what you have just read, especially in this new-age anything-goes society, we assure you that we stand behind our premise. Children are equipped neither emotionally nor intellectually to make decisions beyond their own immediate needs, or to make major or long-range decisions that affect the wellbeing of others. In decision-making, they possess

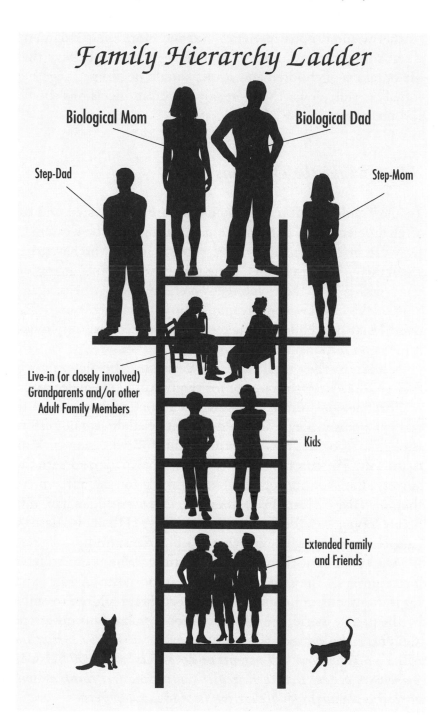

neither wisdom nor experience and therefore their judgment, albeit sometimes accurate, is generally faulty. To believe that the opinions of children and adults should be lumped together equally is ridiculous. Therefore, all important decisions should and must be made by adults.

Adults Make the Decisions

To allow children to voice opinions that are unrequested, and are often unrelenting, is to teach them that they have the wisdom to sway decisions. In our experience, those children who have been given this power are often terrified that their parents are out of touch with reality. These children soon become overwhelmed and burdened by the awesome responsibility of being a "parentified child," that is, a child who takes on adult responsibility when there is no responsible adult to do so.

Children *expect* adults to make decisions. The dichotomy is this: children wish to compete for the power to make decisions, while at the same time recognizing the futility of those wishes to take on a power they really do not want. If adults are not astute enough to recognize the danger in handing over decision-making to immature minds, the children then become strapped with the anxiety that they are somehow responsible for the outcome of their own lives. Most of you will agree that even adults have difficulty coping with the idea of being in charge of their own destiny. Imagine how overwhelming that must be for a child.

Unfortunately, there are some parents who seem to have lost their way. They know about the importance of rules and regulations, and yet, they do not expect their children to abide by them; and worse, they do not enforce them. Our questions are: *Has everyone been taken captive by the permissiveness of the twenty-first century? Are parents under a spell cast by children who want us to believe that their creative spirit and free thinking will be forever damaged if they are confined to social mores?*

In acknowledgement of their creative thinking, we applaud your children's manipulations and their ability to hurl guilt and make it stick. But in reality we must warn you that as a society we are losing our children because they aren't being parented properly. Hence, the dire need for the Hierarchy Ladder.

How The Family Hierarchy Ladder Works

Our Hierarchy Ladder consists of vertical rungs depicting the authority of members or groups in relationship to the other members or groups. For example, in a home with two biologic parents, the top rung of the Family Hierarchy Ladder would be shared equally between mom and dad. Optimally, in this situation, all decisions would be made by their mutual agreement. If there are no other adults residing in this household, such as grandparents, then the rung directly underneath the parents belongs to the children. If grandparents are present, as adults they are to be given respect; their wisdom supersedes the wisdom of children, but does not supersede the decisions made directly by the children's parents; therefore, the grandparents may share the second rung of the ladder, with the children descending to the third rung. Next, in descending order, are rungs for the other extended family members such as aunts and uncles, then friends, then neighbors and so on. If this simple authority structure is followed, there will be order in the family.

The beauty of this Ladder is that each rung remains immobile; regardless of the age of its members, the hierarchy never changes. As your children and step-children mature, they would like to believe that they can up-seat their parents, but the premise of our Family Hierarchy is that even adult children can never ascend to the top rung. That place is always and forever taken by their parents, including those parents who have become quite elderly. Even parents who suffer from dementia or Alzheimer's disease still have lucid moments and often contribute pearls of wisdom. This is not to say that the opinions of individual family members with dementia or Alzheimer's disease are to be followed, but as adults, they are to be given the respect they deserve. Often, within the ramblings of someone with dementia, lucid, factual information is planted.

Where Do Step-Parents Fit?

Where do the step-parents fit on the Family Hierarchy Ladder, since it initially seems as if all the rungs have already been assigned. Once a family is fragmented from divorce fallout, ideally the hierarchy should not change; that is, that even when mom and dad reside in two separate residences, their authority should remain equal and united. In marital dissolution, the parents divorce each other, not their responsibility to parent their children; the rungs of the ladder are strong enough to support and incorporate unity between two separate households.

So again, we need to ask where step-parents belong? Step-parents are such an important aspect in family unification that they almost qualify to stand alongside the biologic parents on the top rung. *Almost.* However, since we have just affirmed that the top rung is reserved only for the biologic parents and cannot be shared by anyone else, we have devised an off-shoot rung, just below the top rung, which belongs to the step-parent. This position is higher than the child's rung, and represents the respect that your step-children owe you as their elders, but still classifies the step-parent separate from the parent.

Some may take this position to be a minimization of your worth and your importance; it is not. This "lesser" physical position is not meant to minimize the worth of the step-parent, but rather to allow time to observe the interactions of the family members without being thrust directly into their space. From this vantage point, step-parents are offered a safe-haven from being accused of "intruding" into the new family, while still being allowed a wide-angle overview of problems and solutions.

Your offshoot rung in the Hierarchy Ladder is flexible, and not immobile like the rest. Your offshoot arms begin to move toward center as your position in the family becomes more secure and less threatening to the children. As you head toward center, you move from your "passive/observing" role to a more assertive role within your blended family.

A Short Course In Family Dynamics

Lesson 1: Timing Is Everything

If you are familiar with our other books, you know that we like to remind you that "timing is everything." This is especially true of step-parenting. No one can blame you for wanting to rush in with your best foot forward, eager to become acquainted with your step-children, hopeful that they will really like you, and that before long you will be fast friends. Yes, this is the goal, but the fastest way to attain that goal is not to rush anywhere, but instead to pace yourself. Your step-children have quite a bit to think about. They have to find a balance in their own emotional world between you and the parent you have "replaced." They have to come to terms with how much of their time with their biologic parent will be taken away by you. They will have to adjust to your curious and unfamiliar ways, including the way you look, talk, cook, laugh, drive, spend leisure time, and so on. You may think this can all be resolved in a few weeks; we like to think more in terms of approximately one year.

You and your new partner may have differences in parenting philosophies. This is not specific to blended families. However, as a new step-parent, you will not be able to share your philosophical input effectively until your "probation" period has passed; then you are no longer at risk of being accused of meddling when you enforce rules or map out boundaries.

Your blended family will need time to adjust, considering all the emotional aspects that impact every member for entirely different reasons. Nonetheless, order cannot be tossed away while the foundation of your new family is settling. Quite the contrary, there are some rules that should be non-negotiable, and universally followed in any family, blended or not, as they are the same regardless of culture, ethnicity or language barriers. For example, the view that children speak respectfully to their elders, which includes anyone in authority, but specifically their parents and step-parents, is foundational. Other rules can be bent or sometimes omitted. Specific to your family, it is you and your spouse who will determine which rules are set in stone and which are primarily "wishful thinking."

About Respect

- Respect is reciprocal; usually when it is given, it is also received.
- Respect relates to boundaries; not only do step-children have to move around within family boundaries, but step-parents also have boundaries, such as honoring privacy and keeping confidences.
- Respect holds sacred those objects from an absent biologic parent and allowing them to be present in the household.
- Respect honors physical and emotional boundaries and does not pry.
- Respect offers a helping hand.
- Respect offers a shoulder to lean (or cry) on.
- Respect cannot be bought, nor manipulated.
- Respect shows no favorites.
- Respect is consistent and fair.
- Respect asks nothing in return.

Lesson 2: Respect Is Foundational

As a step-parent you deserve to be treated with fairness and respect; if your step-children are having difficulty understanding that basic rule, it is your spouse's place to set them straight in no uncertain terms (refer to Strategy #5 for further information).

Respect may have to be earned, but in the beginning, and in the case of brazen, uncivilized, immature, unruly, spoiled or entitled children, *respect will have to be given*, like it or not. Notice that we delegated the task of setting the children straight on the respect issue to your spouse. This was done for two reasons, the first being that there is no need for you to insert yourself into a battlefield when it is not your war. If the children are poorly disciplined, this occurred long before you came on the scene and you should not have to be placed in the line of fire; second, your position is on the offshoot rung of the hierarchy ladder and therefore the bio-logic parent(s) have first crack at making the rules, enforcing them, and issuing consequences for any rules which are not followed; in this case, the rule is respect.

But let's face it, children, especially teenagers, and rules are like oil and water. Nonetheless, in order to properly run the household, certain rules are advantageous to a harmonious existence. Therefore, in step-parenting as in any parenting situation, you are going to have to pick and choose your fights. Although your rung of the ladder still entails a position of authority, it does not automatically allow you to impose your preferences on those below you, or to assume that they agree with your opinions. When and if you get resistance, you may be tempted to "react" rather than simply weighing exactly why you have encountered the resistance. Sometimes, it is not so much that your step-children are arguing a specific point, but rather that they have not truly identified the source of their consternation. For example, a child crying because they cannot bring home a toy from the supermarket may be remembering a time when their absent parent would allow them a "treat" when shopping. In other words, their tears are tears of loss, rather than tears of being spoiled. In times such as these the step-parent has to use his or her powers of acuity, and try to unearth the underlying problem.

However, sometimes a temper-tantrum is simply a temper-tantrum, and therefore must be dealt with through the Behavior-Consequence chart. Please refer back to Lesson 3 for specific information about choosing your fights.

Please do not be insulted, therefore, if your step-children want to refer to you by your given name. This is not a sign of disrespect, but rather a sign of respect to the parent who already wears the name of Mother or Father. We do not espouse the popular concept that step-children should call their step-parents "Mom" or "Dad." First, because you are not their mother or father. This does not hold true, however, if you are the step-parent of an infant or very young child whose biologic parent died or mysteriously disappeared and is unlikely to ever return. Otherwise, unless your step-child specifically asks if they can call you Mom or Dad, it is not only confusing to them for you to make this request, or simply to start doing it, but it is hurtful to their natural parent. Such an assumption on your part may be fueling the fire for a step-child mutiny in your home. Let's see how Chuck made out when he expected his step-son to call him "Dad."

Chuck's Story

Chuck was so upset with his step-son's defiance that he insisted on an emergency meeting at our office. He was angry that ten-year-old Jarrett had refused to follow a clear directive, stating that he was not going to live with a child who was disrespectful without calling for "an all-out war."

Jarrett didn't appear to be disrespectful at all; in fact, he sat quietly while his step-father continued berating him. It seemed that Chuck hadn't had any problems with Jarrett until he married, Claire, Jarrett's biologic mother a few weeks ago. It was during the wedding reception that Chuck told Jarrett he would like to be addressed as "Dad."

Jarrett told his mother he did not want to call Chuck "Dad" but his mother took Chuck's side. Then, in front of one-hundred guests Jarrett blurted out loudly, "I already have a dad, and it isn't you!"

Chuck took Jarrett's outburst personally, and then it became the entire family focus. When, in our office, he finally ended his yelling match, he looked toward us for some alignment. Instead, we explained that Jarrett did have a father, who was very much alive and a part of Jarrett's life. We asked Chuck for an alternate solution to the standoff, but Chuck stood his ground, demanding that we either change our opinion or he would see to it that they went to a therapist who did.

By the look on Claire's face, it was clear that she was pulled in two directions; by the look on Jarrett's face it was clear that his relationship with his step-father was getting a rocky start, with little hope of compromise from this very controlling man.

Lesson 3: Pick and Choose Your Boundary Disputes

Some issues are not worth expending much energy over. Expecting your step-child to volunteer to clean his room is unlikely; no child will recognize the merit of cleanliness regardless of how many lectures you give. This is not to say they should be allowed to live in filth, but if they leave clothes on the floor even though there is a clothes-hamper one foot away, it is to be expected.

At some time in their new family life every step-parent will hear words something like, "You can't tell me what to do; you're not my parent." Your step-children say this type of thing in anger or frustration because they did not expect their life to include divorce, upheaval, drama and change. This declaration is the best defense they can come up with from their bag of tricks. In our experience, they don't mean it.

What is not to be expected, and what merits your immediate energetic attention, is anything in which societal laws are broken; specifically underage drinking, stealing, physical violence and disrespect of law enforcement officers. However, don't bother with the lecture if you drink and drive or dabble in recreational drugs. No matter how you say it, marijuana is an illegal substance and to minimize its illegality is to invite your step-child to the inside of a patrol car.

Personally, we believe in zero tolerance for underage drinking and recreational drugs. Any step-parent who is

Bonding With Your Step-Children

If you really want your step-children to like you, here is a very simple list of things to do. We encourage you to add your own creative thoughts as they come to you through experience.

Be kind to their parent...the one you married. This individual is someone they love and trust, and expect that you will do the same.

Be kind to their parent...the one your spouse divorced. This is an individual whom they also love and trust. Your step-children will appreciate any bridging of emotional upheaval (that chasm opened by divorce shrapnel) you can make by your offering their divorced parent your support.

Be respectful of your step-children's space. This is their safe haven, their area to think, or create, or simply wind down. Allow them that space without interference.

Be interested in what they have to say. They know if you are simply offering lip service, or if every aspect of your body language, eye contact and words invite them to share their thoughts and feelings.

Give them some time to spend with their parent, your spouse, without you. Although they may love spending time with you, they would also like to have their parent's undivided attention at times. They need that one-on-one bonding-time to reassure them that you have not taken their place in their parent's affections.

Stop trying so hard. The only thing your step-children want from you is for you to be genuine. They want you to genuinely be happy to be a part of their family, to genuinely like them, to genuinely be interested in their happiness and welfare, and to genuinely be a good human being.

Let them know that you are not trying to replace their other biologic parent. They need to know this not only by your actions, but also by your words. It is all right to say things like, "I know I'm not your mother, but I still care about your safety," or "I realize I'm not your dad, but I would still like an opportunity to teach you how to drive."

Let them know you like them. First of all, it is perfectly acceptable to say, "I really like (love) you." The degree to which you love them should also be apparent in your laughter, your desire to spend time with them, your display of affection toward them, and your support of them, not only when they do something good, but especially when they haven't made the best choice in a situation.

Be mindful of their feelings...they've been through quite a bit. Their childhood has been temporarily interrupted by divorce, and now remarriage, and the adjustments that are incorporated in those events. Cut them some slack.

Be available. Parents and step-parents alike tend to forget that children are only going to be underfoot for a brief time in the large-scale scheme of things. Sure there are beds to make, floors to clean, work to be dictated, and bills to be paid, but what is most important is standing right next to you, hoping for a moment of your time!

trying to get their step-children to like them by buddying up with a cold beer or a joint is reprehensible and immature. It is illegal as well. The same goes for inviting your step-children's friends to the liquor cabinet because you have secured their car keys and given permission for everyone to spend the night. This not only gives the wrong message, but it is poor judgment. Children are expected to act inappropriately—the still-undeveloped area of their brain houses impulse control. Adult brains are supposed to be fully developed. Which brain do you have?

Lesson 4: Maintain Consistency in Redefining Behavior

Keeping the peace in a house full of children is no easy task, but it can be accomplished by defining your expectations (as we noted at length in the last chapter) in a consistent manner. The key word here is *consistency*. Children can outlast you! In other words, you will wear down long before they do. Therefore, there is no reason to argue with a child of any age. If you are seated properly on your rung of the Family Hierarchy Ladder, you can make a reasonable boundary and expect it to be followed. If not, you can issue a fair consequence. This is hard work. It is easier to just ignore disrespect, but the long-term outcome may cost you quite a bit in time, anguish, therapy bills and even defense attorneys.

Redefining behavior can be done at any stage of development, but the younger your children are the better. As you work to guide them and establish greater clarity about family dynamics, do not give in to manipulation or guilt. Do not feel pressured because you have been goaded into believing you are being unfair in your decisions. Do not give up! Consistency is the key. If you miss one cue, overlook one opportunity to lead by example, or disregard improper behavior don't despair! No parent is perfect, nor are you expected to be. Mistakes are going to be made, situations are going to continue to crop up, and decisions which seem correct one day may give rise to doubt the next. We know you are tired. The whole world is tired. No one is exempt from fatigue, worry, anxiety, stress and exhaustion in this world of ours which seems to be spinning out of control, but this is not an excuse to step-parent ineffectively. Your spouse will hopefully support you, but even if this is not the case, after your "probation" time is completed, at approximately one year, it will be time for you to assert yourself wisely, so that your step-children realize that you will also be giving directives and expecting them to be followed.

Unfortunately, sometimes step-parents unconsciously try to "remake" step-children to become more identifiable to their (the step-parent's) family of origin. Children cannot be remade, but their behavior *can be* redirected; the former has to do with genetic encoding inherited from their biologic parents. If you are looking to disrupt their encoding, you are setting yourself up for failure. You will certainly be an influence as a role model, but wish as you might, your step-children will never be able to share your genetics. However, establishing chores or tasks and enforcing them to be handled responsibly and respectfully has nothing to do with encoding, but rather with compliance.

Lesson 5: Understand Who Is Responsible

In a household, no one person should have to shoulder all the responsibility of running that home, especially if there are some chores that are appropriate for children to do. However, we do not believe a "chore" is defined as work that adults should be doing but don't have to do because they believe in exploiting children. The main job of a child is to go to school, work hard at learning, and understand and apply the concept of socialization. Despite how easy this looks, it is no small feat for a child to master school and friends. This is their *job*, just as you have your job. Nothing that comes under the heading of chores should detract from their school work or necessary playtime.

That said, a list of reasonable and time-limited chores such as clearing the table or emptying the dishwasher is not unreasonable and will teach responsibility on some level. However, since the ideal of learning responsibility is a life-long endeavor, we suggest not making the care for anything that lives and breathes into a chore for your child. This includes feeding the dog, unless it is supervised by you directly; and frankly, if you are going to spend all of your time supervising a chore, you might just as well do it yourself.

The reason that children should not be expected to do housework, laundry or entire lawn maintenance is known as "unfair child labor." To be clear, we believe that adults who have made the decision to bring a child into the world, or take on the role of step-parenting that child, and who assume the ownership of a home, should accept the responsibility of those choices. Children have the responsibility of learning how to follow rules and regulations and eventually matriculate into society someday.

Lesson 6: Draft and Use a Behavior-Consequence Chart
We have already stated our distaste for any manipulation and badgering by your step-children. A behavioral chart can be invaluable in allowing you to set out and enforce consequences without emotions blurring the outcome.

Constructing such a chart should be done during a family meeting, drafted by the adults but assisted by the children. The rules that are laid out should not incorporate generalizations for all children, but should be specific and age-appropriate for each of them. These expectations should be based upon common courtesy and family functioning, and should be drawn up line by line, with each and every parental expectation discussed and then listed in one column, with the adjacent column listing consequences for first time, second time and third time offenses to these line items.

We are not staggering through life wearing rose-colored glasses—we realize that, for the most part, your step-children are not going to be pleased to have their behavior under scrutiny. But, our experience verifies that it will actually benefit them. Once the chart is laid out, they now have the ability to choose to either behave appropriately or face a *known* consequence. Many times, when parents and step-parents have been pushed to their limits, they may make an emotional ruling rather than a clear and logical one. This behavioral chart will keep cool heads and prevent idle threats that serve to minimize the parental credibility. The chart has no favorites and no emotions; the chart cannot be manipulated or forced to change its mind. Further, the chart has been designed with the children's input and understanding. In other words, there has been informed consent given by the children—they understand the expected behaviors of your blended family.

Mike's Story

Mike was a smart child at eight years of age. He knew how to call the police in the case of an emergency; he could recite his address and telephone number; and he knew that no matter how much trouble he got himself into, his step-father would not enforce a punishment.

Peter, his step-father of two years, was considered by most to be impatient and hot-headed; he expected his demands to be met immediately, and he was a stickler for perfection. His unreasonable expectations began trickling down to his step-son Mike, who exhibited sudden anger outbursts and aggressiveness with his school mates.

Peter came into our office for advice on how to discipline Mike, who was clearly pushing the boundaries. One thing we noticed immediately was Peter's impulsive threats; as soon as Mike made an improper choice, Peter's temper (rather than his intellect) dictated the consequence. Later, when he calmed down, the consequence seemed out of sync with the offense, and he either lessened or omitted it.

Mike was a product of Peter's bad temper and his incon-
sistencies in step-parenting; the pattern was emerging. Mike
simply stood victim to Peter's threats, then waited out the
predictable outcome; that is, that no consequence was upheld.
Mike had little respect for Peter's anger or his idle threats.

We helped them craft a Behavior-Consequence chart for
this family, and allowed the chart to dictate the punishment.
Peter was skeptical about the behavior chart, and didn't really
want to use it, but did agree to give it two weeks of consistent
usage. It wasn't long before his step-son saw his egregious acts
cross-referenced to inevitable outcomes in black and white;
because there were no loopholes with which to maneuver
his manipulations, Mike began changing his behavior. Mike
learned that he could not control this family, and Peter learned
that the written word is a powerful tool.

Sample Behavior-Consequence Charts

As in all aspects of parenting, nothing is written in cement. The
content of this chart is at the discretion of the adults who drafted
it—with extenuating circumstances, it is their prerogative to alter
any aspect of the "crime" or the "punishment." Remember, it is not
for your step-children to decide if you have treated them fairly; they
will almost always believe you have not. But, if you know that you
have based your decision impartially, then enforce it confidently.

Sample Chart for Jason, age 6

Disrespect:
- Offense #1, verbal warning
- Offense #2, time out, one minute
- Offense #3, time out, two minutes
- Recurrent offense, no cartoons Saturday morning

Fighting with Siblings:
- Offense #1, verbal warning
- Offense #2, time out, 2 minutes
- Recurrent Offense, cannot play with siblings for 1 hour.

Sample Chart for Trisha, age 14

Disrespect:
- Offense #1, verbal warning
- Offense #2, loss of iPod for the day
- Recurrent Offense, loss of cell phone and iPod for two days
- Continued Ongoing Offenses, loss of all privileges and electronic devices for 48 hours.

Lying:
- Offense #1, loss of privileges and grounding for one day
- Offense #2, loss of privileges and grounding for one week
- Continued ongoing offense, loss of all privileges, and all electronic devices including computer until further notice

Fighting With Siblings:
- Offense #1, verbal warning
- Offense #2, loss of phone privilege for one night
- Continued ongoing offense: loss of privileges and all electronic devices (cell phone, iPod, etc.) until further notice.

Some of you may agree with us in theory, but believe that you are unable to enforce the discipline you have written on the chart. This is not the time to act helplessly. If you have lost control of your step-children, or your blended family, we have to stop ourselves from shouting, "How could you have let this happen?" Come on folks, get a grasp on what's at stake here. You are teaching right and wrong; this is the job you signed up for. It's too late to turn back now.

If you want compliance from your step-children all you have to do is say these four magic words: "I own your stuff!" That's right! You do own their stuff, and that power of ownership is about to change your life. Are you getting the picture yet? They own nothing. They love their stuff, and yet, they own none of it. You do. Even those things that may have been purchased with saved-up birthday money or allowance do not constitute items that "belong" to them. They were *allowed* the privilege of purchasing that item for their pleasure under the guidelines set forth by you; these guidelines should indicate that if rules are not complied with, then even those items purchased with their own money become subject to confiscation.

Your step-children have the right to a safe environment, food on the table, clothing, and a place to rest their head at night. Their claim to the material possessions in your home, including the cell phone, is an illusion created in their minds; and you have been brainwashed to go along with this illusion. Wake up! Their cell phone, iPod, computer, automobile, television and anything else you can think of, is owned by you and loaned to them. Unless they are paying the mortgage, utility bills, and credit card bills, their stuff is really your stuff!

Johnny's Story

Johnny always had a problem following rules made by adults; ever since he was in the third grade he spent day after day in the principal's office, sent there by his teachers who were fed up at his rebellious attitude. That attitude really escalated by the time Johnny reached puberty, and after being suspended from school for cheating on a test, Johnny was brought into our office for evaluation.

At first he was smug, refusing to give us any respect or acknowledgment, but he quickly realized that although he might have been able to control his family with his antics, he was not in any position to control our office. We had no emotional ties to Johnny, which of course alleviates any guilt felt by some adults when their child is punished. But also, we had the confidence to know that we would be victorious in achieving positive results from Johnny's new behavior once we established that he was no longer calling the shots. We allowed him to verbalize his indignation at being told what to do by his parents, as well as any gripes he had with his family. Essentially, the only gripe he could come up with was that he did not like being told what to do.

After we constructed the behavior chart, he realized that although he did not agree with any of it, he was going to have to follow it to the letter when everything that Johnny owned (with the exception of his bed, necessary clothing and school work) was bagged up and removed from the house to an undisclosed location. The more unbearable his attitude became, the longer the amount of time before he actually saw his things returned, one by one. It took him two months to fully understand that he could not win; after that realization, he simply gave up and did what he was expected to do with a pleasant attitude. Every so often he regresses and must be "reminded" by coming home from school to find an object "missing," but it isn't long before he is right back on track.

Nothing will persuade your step-children to be respectful and follow rules than to lose what they believe they are entitled to; you not only have a right to take their things away if they cannot obey the rules of the house, you have a duty to take them if that is the only method that will teach them exactly how the Family Hierarchy Ladder works.

Remember, the beauty of this chart is not to hold your step-children hostage to your demands, but to clearly remind them to learn how to make better choices. It also reminds you just who is running your household.

Lesson 7: Protect Your Children—At Home and Everywhere Else

Blended families, like any families, are made up of individuals with unique character and personality traits. Within these subset-traits are those identified as weaker and stronger. The weaker individuals often need protecting from those stronger, until their physical abilities and self-esteem catch up. Whether you are the step-parent or the biologic parent, do not expect your children to endure bullying or harassment, even if it is from their own siblings. If you would not allow your child to be tortured by a stranger, you should protect him or her from the same type of treatment in their own home.

In our sample chart, you might have noticed that we insist that siblings are given as much respect as adults. There are many schools of thought on siblings and step-siblings not getting along, or competing with each other, but in this twenty-first century, fighting among siblings can have devastating consequences. Unlike a quick punch in the nose that settled battles just a few decades ago, this behavior is now considered assault, which in fact it is, with the result being the possibility of a skull fracture or worse. Today's youth carry anger and stress that is almost palpable. With parental/academic expectations, minimum-wage employment, mental and physical fatigue, grueling schedules, experimentation with drugs and alcohol, inappropriate erotic material and premature sexual experiences, Internet dangers, splintered families and unsupervised time, your step-children have quite a bit to be concerned about.

Current brain research indicates that kids through the chronologic age of twenty-three are unequipped emotionally, mentally or physically to make consistently good decisions. Consequently, it is not only street-children and gang members who find themselves in predicaments that can potentially ruin their lives. Society's children, your children, may be only one weapon away from prison time; the victim of aggression may be only one altercation away from permanent neurological impairment.

You should not encourage your step-children to fight their own battles with their siblings, or turn a blind eye when they do. It is your duty as a step-parent to monitor those accusations, tantrums, aggressions, verbal insults and physical assaults that can cause irreparable emotional and physical damage.

James's Story

James had always been bullied by his biologic brothers. He was the youngest of three boys, with a thin frame like that of his mother. He was such an easy target that his mother, Stephanie, almost couldn't recall a time when he wasn't being teased or pushed around by his siblings. When Stephanie remarried, her husband Bruce was appalled to observe James's plight. "I realize I'm only the step-father," he said, "and I haven't been one for long, but I believe it is my moral obligation to protect this child." He was correct.

James agreed to enter therapy to talk about the sibling rivalry going on in his family. By the time he had "relived" and recounted many of the events, we were fast approaching labeling it abusive. He spent weeks talking about his humiliation and sadness that his brothers didn't like him. His mother tried to convince James that the attention he was getting from his brothers was "affectionate" in a male-kind of way. Bruce, the step-father, corrected her before we had a chance, though we agreed with his estimation. He said, "Honey, I know you want to believe that, because it makes it easier for you to accept that your son has been bullied right under your nose for a long time, but wishing it was something else doesn't change the facts."

Bruce was a strong step-father presence, and had come into James's life just when he needed him most. Bruce tried to enlist the assistance of the children's biologic father, but this man was uninterested and unavailable. Since Stephanie was too weak to deal with her sons at this time, Bruce stepped in and began structuring new boundaries for the family. Although this vignette does not follow our suggestion to step back for the first year as a step-parent, there are always exceptions and this case was one of them.

As anticipated, the other boys were less than pleased by their step-father's interference. They had a good thing going until he began enforcing rules that confined their freedom. Bruce was less concerned about his popularity than with protecting a child who could otherwise not protect himself. He also enrolled James in Karate classes so that he would never feel intimidated by anyone again. Although he invited his other step-sons to enroll as well, to date they have declined his offer.

Bruce did the right thing under extreme circumstances, and the family will continue in therapy until all their issues are resolved and Bruce has been accepted by all members of the family.

Feeling safe in one's own home is not a privilege, but a right; that includes emotional as well as physical safety. Any rivalry that you observe to be unrelenting, unfair, or at the expense of the other person requires your immediate action. We often speak with both parents and step-parents who profess to be shielded under the umbrella of ignorance; common phrases from them include, "I wasn't there," or "I didn't see it." Pretending that you are unaware of what goes on underneath your own roof should be so embarrassing that you wouldn't dare utter such nonsense. If your step-children need your help, please come to their rescue, not tomorrow, but today, because waiting too long is often … waiting too long! Children commit suicide; what one child may be able to endure, another cannot. Children who are picked on, bullied, harassed or humiliated often make impulsive and tragically permanent choices.

Lesson 8: Listen Listen Listen

Listening to your step-children is paramount to good communication. The obvious way a person listens to someone is through their hearing, but effective listening includes so much more.

For instance, your step-child might be saying things are going all right in school, but your intuition tells you that is not so. It may be the way he physically slumps over his dinner plate, or the way she drags her feet walking home from the school bus. In other words, body language is giving clues that something is wrong.

Rather than saying "How was your day?" you might elicit a more honest answer by saying something like, "You seem a little forlorn. Something must have happened at school today. Can you tell me about it?" The second example does two things: it announces that you already are aware your step-child has something on his or her mind, and it communicates that you are interested in listening to what the problem is.

If your step-child does not want to talk about a problem, rather than grilling them, which will only push a child farther into a shell, you might say, "Well, it sounds like you need some time to think things over. When you are ready, I would be happy to sit down and talk about this with you." Then, be sure to make the time to listen, and do not "pry" at a time when your step-child has shut down. After they process as best they can, remind them again that they can share their feelings with you.

Most of all, good listening is non-judgmental, so don't jump in with opinions and judgments, especially if they are about friends; children make up with their friends quickly and do not really want the "litter" of knowing that you never liked them anyway!

STRATEGY #4

"Make Nice" With the Former Spouse

In case you haven't noticed, there is an elephant in the room, and that elephant is going to have to be addressed. We are speaking, of course, of your partner's former spouse—the other biologic parent.

While you may prefer to pretend that your spouse had no former life before you came into the picture, this rarely works for very long. In fact, not only did your spouse have a life prior to you, but there are children as proof. Further, we are going to have to be the bearers of bad news: your partner and the former spouse did, at least once, have sex.

This is not good news to think about, process or digest. However, this information needs to be forefront if you are going to be able to identify and then resolve any emotions about your spouse's former partner. Why is this necessary? Because this Strategy #4 invites you to do something difficult—to "make nice" with the other biologic parent, if you haven't already done so.

Things in Perspective

Although it may be distasteful to think about your spouse and his former partner in the throes of intimacy, may we remind you that they are not intimate now. Further, regard-less of which partner actually filed the paperwork for divorce, at least one if not both partners recognized that the trust, love and commitment that it takes to make a marriage work was missing in their marriage. If you are jealous of your spouse's former spouse because of reality-based factors, it is worth spending a few sessions with a therapist to help you with resolution. However, if you are envious of your spouse's past, and live in some alternate universe where your spouse was celibate until the day you met him or her, then we must speak to that part of your personality that has not fully found its way past adolescence. We say to you, with the utmost respect ... grow up!

You need to get a grip on your insecurities. Surely they have not just surfaced at this juncture of your life. This is the time for introspection; dig deep and find out what lures you down that path of jealousy and bring the issues to the surface. Take this opportunity to evaluate your feelings of inferiority and seek resolution. Your spouse is going to have to relate to his or her former spouse regularly about the children. Wouldn't you rather be a part of that communica-tion than an outsider, which is where your insecurities are going to put you?

The **Personal Revelation Chart** that follows is our tool to help you get to your true feelings about the former spouse. Sometimes, the written word illuminates more clearly the obstacles that stand in the way of your acceptance of any-thing. This Chart is not for public display, but rather to be useful to you personally. Please add a page in your journal for this important exercise, and try to answer as many ques-tions as you care to, with as much insight as you can, for the best results. The outcome of this self-exploration may be surprising to you, in a good way. Once you pinpoint your barriers to relationship, you can more easily work on chip-ping away at them.

Your Personal Revelation Chart

- I don't want to know the former spouse because ...
- I don't trust the former spouse because ...
- I am jealous of the former spouse because ...
- When I hear my spouse talking with his/her "ex" on the telephone it makes me ...
- I think my spouse still wishes to be back with his/her ex because ...
- Reasons I dislike the former spouse:
- Reasons the former spouse doesn't like me:
- Reasons the former spouse doesn't trust me:
- Gossip that the former spouse has said about me:
- Gossip that I have said about the former spouse:
- I am willing (not willing) to make amends and try again to interact with the former spouse because ...
- I think my step-children compare me to their other biologic parent because ...
- I feel that I can never measure up to the former spouse because ...
- I have spoken (not spoken) to my spouse about my feelings because ...
- Speaking (or not speaking) to my spouse about my feelings has resulted in ...

We know that facing these issues isn't easy. No one wants to be scrutinized by the other parent, or disliked solely because that marriage didn't work and this marriage does, but someone is going to have to make an effort to really blend this family, and that means every member, past and present. Some of your insecurities may be factual. Perhaps your weight is at issue, or your experience; maybe the former spouse had more education or a better career. Those are things you can change or accept. But what about your irrational insecurities—the ones that lurk around the bedroom when you wonder if you measure up; the ones that play tricks with your sensibility when you feel certain your spouse wishes he or she had never gotten divorced. Nothing can convince someone that irrational thoughts *are* irrational, other than laying out the facts and continuing to face them bravely.

Facts to Remember

Fact 1: Your spouse is not with the former spouse because they differed on ideas, philosophies, interests or the ability to have fun together.

Fact 2: There was either a trust issue, a sexual issue, or a compatibility issue in the former marriage that caused its collapse.

Fact 3: Your spouse married you because his or her divorce signified the end of the previous marriage and the end of any intimate relationship with that former partner. When we say *intimate*, we are not merely inferring sexually intimate, but intimate with secrets, feelings, dreams, hurts or confidences.

Fact 4: If you continue to throw your insecurities into your new marriage, you are inviting not only trouble, but the former spouse back into the relationship, courtesy of you.

There is no competition between you and the former spouse. By using the word "competition" you are inferring that there is a competitor; there is not. But just for the record, if this was a competition, you would have already won, with the grand prize coming home to you each night, eating at your dinner table and sleeping in your bed.

Give yourself and your spouse a break. If you want to be the person your spouse trusts implicitly, the one he turns to with his fears, the one she turns to with her intimate insecurities, don't get bogged down in the minutia of the past. This is your moment, your time, your new family. This is the rest of your life, so choose wisely because the rest of your life starts now.

If you can allay the anxieties you might have that are based on any romantic illusions concerning your spouse and his/her ex, you will be more inclined to do two things more easily: first, to meet the other biologic parent and try to interact on friendly terms; second, to allow your spouse to interact with the former partner without any snide remarks or paranoia from you.

First things first. Some of you may not be new to your spouse's former spouse, especially if you all live in the same town. Those who live in a metropolitan area might not have been introduced before, even if you both find yourselves living in the same apartment building. If you *do* know each other but are not on civil terms, one of you is going to have to make a move toward civility. We hope that will be you.

Meeting the Former Spouse

If the other biologic parent is entirely unknown to you, it behooves you to meet as soon as possible. That parent is certainly going to be curious and also concerned as to your character traits and parenting philosophy. If you want the natural parent to warm up to you without feeling threatened, be accessible and agreeable. She or he will be somewhat reassured if you don't have a criminal rap sheet, but on a deeper level they will be assessing your mood, temperament, attitude, general warmth and congeniality, and your level of commitment and compassion toward their children. Remember, if you are ill at ease, they are terrified; they are entrusting their most precious gift into your care.

From the outset, realize that you and the other parent have one thing in common—your step-children. Let them know your parenting philosophy, especially if you have children of your own. If not, let them know that you love children and want to work harmoniously with those approaches to parenting prevailing thus far. It is important for them to know how much you value honesty, integrity, truthfulness and respect. Offer to encourage your step-children to call or visit as frequently as possible, showing the natural parent that you are not a "substitute" for them, but rather an adjunct to the family unit.

Renee's Story

Renee hated Olivia, though the two had never met. Nonetheless, as soon as Renee discovered her former husband was going to marry someone half her age, she went on a rampage. One night Olivia overheard her soon-to-be step-children telling their father unflattering stories about her, and was hurt to think that this woman whom she had never met was so bent on destroying her relationship with the children. Richard, a level-headed man who rarely acted on emotions, knew that a meeting where both women could confront each other was the only logical way to set things straight. He counted on the fact that the images that both women had of the other would be worse than what they would actually discover. Richard was correct.

Although neither woman looked forward to the meeting, they both appeared dressed extravagantly from head to toe. Within minutes the facades gave way to genuine caring about the children, expressions of feelings of inadequacy from each of them, and a desire to help each other forge their new roles. By the end of an hour, they both eagerly exchanged phone numbers and agreed to meet again.

Understanding Biologic Loss

Why should you go out of your way to work with the other parent? *Because it is the right thing to do.* If your step-children live with you full time, or fifty percent of the time, the natural parent may feel as though they have "lost" their children in some respects. This feeling of loss often precipitates otherwise intelligent parents to react in an uncharacteristic manner—like uttering innuendos or outright lies to try to sway the children to align themselves with the injured parent. Even if your step-children visit infrequently, it is a comfort to the natural parent to know that the person who is tucking their children in bed for the night is concerned about their happiness and welfare.

We cannot discount the influence that the other biologic parent has upon their children, especially if they view themselves to be the "jilted" partner, meaning that, although they may have been divorced for quite some time, once you arrive in the equation they become territorially threatened. If they see you as their "replacement," all semblance of rational thinking gives way to shards of irrational behavior.

Therefore, we stress meeting the other biologic parent as soon as possible in the hope that you can create a parenting team. If you or your spouse are unwilling to support this effort, be prepared for a very rocky road; it is this type of standoff that forces your step-children to choose sides. Generally speaking, it is unlikely that *your side* will be chosen. Loyalty to the biologic parent is just too strong. Conversely, children are relieved when they observe their biologic parents and step-parents interacting in a friendly manner; it teaches forgiveness, caring, compassion, fairness and a genuine desire to put your step-children's needs at the forefront.

Keep Trying!

We know this is not a perfect world, and that sometimes even the best intentions and humble approaches fall flat. Keep trying. You may not be received with the same degree of warmth and enthusiasm that you have offered, but even neutral dialogue is a stepping off point. You have little control over the manner in which the other natural parent treats you, but you do have control over your own behavior. At all times you must be in control of your temper, and be respectful, keeping in mind that it is not the spoken word, but the manner in which it is spoken, that makes all the difference.

One of the quickest ways to turn even a good relationship bad is to come across as a "know it all." Perhaps your parenting expertise has proven better than that of the former spouse, and perhaps their involvement with their own children is marginal at best. That is not a signal for you to march in with tips and opinions. Remember, being right most of the time is better than being right some of the time, and being right all of the time is just plain wrong!

In the story that follows, Margaret almost ruined her relationship with Melanie, the other biologic parent, by knowing everything.

Margaret's Story

Nothing irritated Melanie more than her children's new step-mother Margaret, or more specifically the attitude that Margaret carried with her like a badge of honor. Initially, Melanie was pleased that Simon was remarrying; he had been single for the past ten years and still he seemed cautious with the girls when they came to visit him, as if he needed female input to close the gender gap. Margaret seemed to share similar philosophies about parenting, with an uncanny ability to size up situations and keep one step ahead of her precocious teens.

Margaret immediately won over Melanie's confidence by showing up at parent/teacher meetings and after-school activities. She was actively involved in almost every aspect of the girls' personal and academic lives within months. After six months she was all but telling everyone what to do. By criticizing the teachers and putting neighbors on the defensive, it seemed that Margaret believed no one was capable of raising the girls except herself; that unspoken inference included Melanie.

Melanie came into our office seeking advice about communication skills. She very much wanted to keep a good relationship with Margaret, but wanted to remind her that her views were not the only views. We explained the Family Hierarchy Ladder to Melanie, and asked if she would mind sharing the next meeting with Margaret. One week later both women came in. We had drawn a Ladder depicting the top rung as Melanie and Simon's; Margaret's rung was below, and still off-center, having not been married long enough to move toward the middle. Margaret seemed offended at first, as if she had been demoted, but before long she understood that although she possessed excellent advice *most* of the time, this family had been used to working together in a synchronized fashion; and part of that synchrony was to quietly approach teachers and neighbors if there were problems, rather than creating a scene.

To everyone's surprise, Margaret actually felt relieved that she didn't have to work so hard at proving that she was a good step-parent. She was simply trying to find her place in her new role, and the more she had tried, the more her desperation had increased, until she sensed that no matter what she did, someone was either finding fault or withdrawing. Margaret took a very courageous step. She admitted that, because of her desire to be recognized as a good step-mother, she had overstepped her bounds. The one thing she wanted most, credibility, had almost backfired due to her insecurities.

Difficult Communications

As always, communication is key with any relationship; hence the importance of being able to speak openly with your spouse and the other biologic parent about each other's strengths and weaknesses.

Finding common ground with the other biologic parent poses one set of problems, but even after that, things are still not going to run smoothly all the time. Gossip, misinformation and lies will present you with some serious communications challenges. For example, your step-children may come to you with information that is unfounded and based in gossip, especially if you haven't been accepted in the blended family by their natural parent. In these instances you need to rise above the fray and keep your wits about you. Losing control and reacting when you are accused of something that is unfair and unfounded is only going to confirm a reason to validate the gossip.

For example, let's assume that your step-children tell you that their natural parent has slandered your name and inferred that you were the "home-wrecker" and the underlying reason for the divorce. Whether or not this is accurate, partly accurate, or completely untrue, none of this should be discussed with your step-children other than to make a statement that upholds your innocence, if you are innocent. The tone used by your step-children may tell you whether they are concerned, or angry, or both; they believe they have a duty to defend their biologic parent from humiliation and anguish. It does no one any good to call the other parent a liar, even though that is probably what you would like to do. Instead, you have a right to give basic factual information in response to slanderous material, without accusation or emotion. Until the age of reason, your step-children would rather believe lies from their parents than truths from their step-parents. Remember, if you fall into the mud with your opponent, you will both slosh around in filth.

Sometimes, it is not that the other biologic parent doesn't want to befriend you, but rather because of your insecurity you have spoken ill about them. If that is the case, you will undoubtedly be labeled as an officious meddler, or simply put, a troublemaker. You may also be accused of attempting to alienate that parent from the family circle for your own secondary gains. In most cases, we would concur. Eventually, even the most loyal step-child finally accepts their parent for the immature, deceptive and uncooperative individual he or she really is. Unfortunately, once the truth is no longer hidden, acting-out behaviors and depression, in the children, follow close behind.

Another useful strategy is to say something that negates the gossip without going into detail. Suppose the children are reporting gossip relating to adultery or any other serious matter. One of the best statements of your innocence would be to simply say, "I love your father (mother) very much and I would never do anything to hurt him (her). I would also never do anything to hurt you. I am sorry that you have been given information that has confused you." This will reassure your step-children that you are not going to slander their other parent. It also indicates that you have nothing to hide.

Betty's Story

Betty sought therapy because she was unable to control her impulses to attack the character of Theresa, the new step-mother. In fact, before she even met Theresa, she managed to dig up as much "dirt" on her as she could; what she couldn't find she fabricated. Her slander did nothing to enhance her standing to her former husband Tom or his new wife, but in the interest of the children, Tom and Theresa chose to ignore the gossip Betty was promoting around town.

When Betty began her campaign to smear Theresa to the children, both Tom and Theresa had no choice but to take a stand. Theresa's step-children were refusing to come to the house because their mother had called her a "home-wrecker" and told them in detail, albeit fabricated detail, of exactly how Theresa managed to "steal" their father away. We explained to Betty that none of this would do the children any good, but she was so invested in revenge and hatred that she continued her slander. Thirty days later she found herself in family court facing a custody battle. The judge gave her another thirty days to stop alienating the children from their father's home, but she could not control her impulses to hurl nasty accusations at every turn. As a final result, the court gave permanent custody to Tom and Theresa. The judge believed that they would offer the children a healthier emotional environment in which to grow and develop.

Setting Things Straight

Step-children often unload their parent's comments about their step-parents, even in its most inaccurate form. Loretta hadn't been a step-mother for very long before she engaged in a conversation with her step-children that enlightened all of them.

Loretta's Story

Loretta instituted "family time" with her step-children as they cleaned the dinner dishes and loaded the dishwasher. One particular evening her step-children brought up the topic of Loretta's poverty-filled upbringing. Loretta was shocked at the idea that her step-children portrayed her in this manner; when she asked what had driven them to believe such a thing, the oldest step-son answered, "Mama said you were trailer park trash."

It took every ounce of will power within her not to rush to the telephone and call their mother a liar, but instead, she found the wisdom to teach her step-children a lesson about patience in a non-judgmental way. She began, "There are many people in this world who aren't as fortunate as we are, but they are decent, hard-working people just the same. They go to work, cook and clean, love their babies, and do the best they can, just like we do. Some people do that in a big house like this, and some people do it in a trailer, but we're all the same, just living in different places."

Her step-children thought about what Loretta said and then questioned why their mother told them that. Loretta was kind in her response. "Your mother must have been mistaken. I never lived in a trailer, although come to think of it, it might have been fun, don't you think?"

Fortunately not all former spouses want revenge; they simply want the truth. If you are speaking with the parent directly, an effective communication strategy is to begin by acknowledging the other's hurt or outrage, while you reinforce your own integrity and then invite the angry other to help you. With the very rare exception, most former spouses will "come around" once they have recognized that unification is best for everyone. In order to present yourself in a non-threatening light you might say something such as, "I understand your mistrust of me after the gossip that has filtered throughout the town, but I want you to know that it is untrue. I have more respect for myself, and your family, than to casually disregard your children in this way. I don't know what we can do to stop it, but I certainly wish I did."

It serves no purpose to defend yourself to the other biologic parent, especially if the gossip has been promoted through the grapevine. If it has been promoted directly by the parent, facing them head-on in a credible manner can do quite a bit to put out the fire. If this gossip was told to you by your step-children, having come directly from their parent, there is no need to mention the source; doing so will simply cause a problem for your step-children and encourage their mistrust of you.

If you believe your step-children are "fishing" to see how much you might know about ugly inferences made about you, do not pry. Your step-children are going to proceed with caution, unsure of how you will react to negative information. If you listen in a non-judgmental, non-emotional manner it is likely they will come to you with more at a later date. If your step-children withhold information, give them time; it is rare that your step-child will not come forward sooner or later, depending on how much they feel they can trust you to remain in control. Most of all, they don't want to get into trouble with their other parent by being a "snitch."

For older step-children who need more information from you, give them the circumstantial facts. If the accusation concerns impropriety or deliberate "house-wrecking," for example, an honest time-frame may help: "Your father and I met at a seminar last July in Atlanta, Georgia. At first we shared a business lunch, but when we realized we had quite a bit in common personally, we began dating. This was eight months (one year, three years) following your parent's divorce." Time frames do not work, however, if you already were acquainted with your spouse while he or she was still married, regardless of how innocent you are.

It may be true that you were acquainted with your current spouse prior to the divorce of the former spouse, and it is also possible that you may, in fact, have engaged romantically with your current spouse prior to the divorce of the former spouse. If so, this is not for public consumption, *and* there is no reason to be indignant about rumors. There is something about protesting too much! Each situation is unique and therefore your responses will have to be adjusted accordingly, but you will certainly help to keep your integrity intact regardless of the accusations by not becoming defensive or angry. Most situations are easily defused and set aside when an adequate explanation is offered.

If there has been infidelity, which has been proven so, no explanation is going to soothe feelings or make the children accept that their parent has stepped outside the marriage sexually or emotionally. Some parents choose to tell their children that their needs were not being met by the other parent, but we do not consider this appropriate. There are some issues that should not be discussed in detail with children, regardless of their age; and infidelity, we believe, is one. However, in "proven cases" or cases where a parent has confessed to being a participant to adultery with an individual who is now their step-parent, damage control becomes damage salvage. In other words, be prepared to have your children angry, acting out, and resentful of both you and their step-parent. This is unfortunate, but is also to be expected. Time and love will help them heal. But remember, children are very protective of a parent-victim—who in situations such as these will be the other biological parent—regardless of any defense you might want to make. The only stance you should take is to express sorrow for having placed everyone involved in such a situation, and to ask for forgiveness. Stay positive and continue to love your children and step-children as they adjust to this very painful and humiliating issue.

Once you and your spouse's former partner have formed a bond based upon your mutual dedication to the children, you can agree to communicate regularly as to any achievements or punishments that have occurred. As quickly as children's lives change, this communication might be several times each week. Often, if your relationship is based on caring and honesty, you might be surprised to find that the other biologic parent would prefer to speak with *you* directly, rather than to their former spouse. This is fine. As long as your step-children are the beneficiaries of open communication, it doesn't matter who passes the information along.

Bridging the Gap

Your step-children need both their biologic parents in their lives; children were designed to be raised by more than one parent, contrary to the popular belief that when divorce became fashionable and the single-household was born, the kids would be just fine. Leaving a spouse behind is one thing, but leaving a child behind is quite another. As a step-parent you are poised to help bridge the gap between the biologic parents.

You are not in competition with the other biologic parent. It is only logical than neither household will agree on every parenting issue; bedtime at one house might be rigidly structured while at another it is lackadaisical and unstructured. Curfews, mealtimes, homework schedules and leisure time may also be vastly different, but that really doesn't have to be confusing to children once they understand that what Mom expects to be followed *at her house* is not necessarily what Dad expects to be followed in his. As a step-parent, there is no need for you to get caught up in an emotional battle because you believe their bedtime is incorrect at the other house. As we discussed within Strategy #3, choose your battles carefully. If you are looking for trouble, you won't have to go far before you find it.

Different Lifestyles ... But Always Safe

You are entitled to your opinions about lifestyle differences, but share your opinions only with your spouse, and confidentially, or better yet, keep them to yourself. In the big scheme of life, it isn't going to matter that your step-children eat fast food three nights a week at the other household. If you are a health food advocate, then serve them healthy food when they are at your house and be done with it. That is all you can do. If you are unsettled because your step-children prefer take-out pizza over your homemade hummus, that is to be expected; their judgments are immature and based upon immediacy. Just do the best you can, and allow the other parent to do the best he or she can, whether you agree or not.

Only when there is a safety issue should you speak up, and then by all means speak loudly. By "safety issue" we do not mean that your step-children are sometimes allowed to stay awake past midnight and you are concerned about their lack of sleep. We are speaking about leaving young children home unattended, or allowing them to ride in automobiles without using their safety restraints. Other issues may include dropping them off to spend the night unsupervised at a home of a mere acquaintance, or serving alcohol to minors when their adolescents have a party. Anything that impacts their immediate safety or health, or poses a threat of abuse or loss of life must be dealt with immediately and swiftly. This is one time that as a step-parent, even if your blended family is relatively new, you can up-seat yourself from the offshoot arm of the hierarchy ladder and scramble to the top rung until the danger has passed.

Most step-parents will rarely find themselves in a situation where their step-children's safety is at issue because of the negligence of the biologic parent (either of them). Mostly, there will simply be differences of opinions as to how each household functions. What the other natural parent decides to do in his or her home may differ from your parenting philosophy, but if we review the Family Hierarchy Ladder, their position on the top rung trumps yours.

Access Granted

As a rule of thumb, unless the other biologic parent is a serial killer or sexual predator, your step-children have a desire, a need, and more importantly a right to uninterrupted and uncontaminated access to both parents. Even the most dysfunctional biologic parent has the support and love of his or her children; anyone who tries to come between them is employing poor judgment. Remember, every human being has lessons to teach, even those which are taught through character flaws.

As a step-parent you have taken on the responsibility of raising your step-children in the best way you know how, and that means even when you don't feel like it, you owe them enough restraint to at least pretend to respect their natural parent.

Brian's Story

Brian could never stand Allen from the day they met. Allen drank too much, smoked heavily, and essentially spent most of his days getting by with doing as little as possible. When Brian became the step-father to Allen's children, he used their father as a prime example of what *not to become* when they grew up. He made fun of Allen in front of the children and made it a point to illuminate his laziness. When Allen was arrested for drinking and driving, Brian was elated. He was trying hard to make an impression on his step-children, which he certainly did, but not in the way he had hoped.

Allen's sons, ages twelve and fourteen, were disappointed in their father, but kept hoping that one day he would make a decision to change. It seemed to them that Brian relished their father's poor decisions, which made them feel embarrassed as well as angry. They didn't need anyone to tell them that their father was a loser. The whole neighborhood already did that. What they needed was a sympathetic shoulder to lean on, and an adult who would support their hopes in their Dad's change one day.

It didn't take long before the boys didn't want to hang around Brian anymore. Instead, they began aligning themselves with their father, believing that if no one else was going to stand by him, they would. Soon both boys began role-modeling some of Allen's bad habits; when Dad lit up a cigarette, they lit up as well. When Dad went into the refrigerator for a beer, he took out three, one for him and one for his "new-found friends." If only Brian hadn't pushed his step-children over to Allen's defense, things might have unfolded differently. As of this writing, the boys don't want much to do with their step-father, who continues to publicly berate their father.

Strategies to Help Bond With The Other Spouse

- Ask your spouse to set up a face to face meeting between you and the former spouse.
- Introduce yourself in a friendly, non-threatening manner.
- Ask the former spouse to assist you in getting to know your step-children from their (the former spouse's) perspective.
- Explain that you would like to be able to "count" on the other spouse's assistance in helping you to understand the children's personality, quirks, attitudes, likes and dislikes.
- Explain that the more you understand the former spouse's parenting philosophies, the better able you will be to incorporate those same philosophies in your household, if they are similar to your own.
- Tell the former spouse you would like to regularly communicate, and ask if there could be a weekly scheduled phone exchange to go over the events of that week.
- Ask if the former spouse would like you to ensure that the children, while at your home, call their parent for a daily or nightly check-in.
- Let the former spouse know if their child said something especially nice about him or her. Or relay a story in which the child referred to the former spouse in a kindly manner.
- Keep the former spouse informed about academic and social information pertaining to your step-children, such as school awards, tardiness or absenteeism, teacher conferences, school plays, school trips, and illnesses.
- Invite the former spouse to any events that you hold in your step-children's honor, such as birthday parties, graduation events, or holiday parties.

- Inform the former spouse if there are behavioral prob-lems that you are observing at your home, and inquire about whether you can elicit their assistance with these issues.
- Ask if there are any consequences for behavior problems at the former spouse's home that should be carried over into your home, such as being grounded for a weekend, or loss of use of the car for one week, etc.
- Tell the former spouse that you do not intend to "cover" for your step-children; this aligns you with the other parent in honesty and integrity. For example, if the children do not want to speak to the former spouse when called, you can nicely but truthfully explain that the child refused to pick up the telephone, rather than lie about them being in the shower.
- Most of all, let the former spouse know that you are willing and desirous of "teaming up" with them to find resolution to any problems that may arise.

P.S.—*Close Enough Is … Close Enough*

Some of you may find that you not only get along well with the former spouse, but that you would like to have a close friendship with this person, independent of the former mar-riage and all that it entails. We do not endorse this sentiment, as it almost always leads to jealousy and comparisons at some juncture. Rather, keep the newfound friendship at a "close dis-tance" to insure that the overall family relationship continues as smoothly as possible.

STRATEGY #5
Create a Parenting Partnership

Step-parenting is not a single act, but rather a team effort. Although the primary purpose of this book is to assist *you* with step-parenting, your spouse is the other half of your step-parenting team. It is he or she who will guide you along your newly-cleared path as you become more confident in the step-parenting role; without his or her support, your step-children are more likely to offer more resistance to your step-parenting goals. Especially if you aren't getting much assistance from the other biologic parent, and you aren't winning any popularity contests with your step-children, then the person you *most* need in your corner is your spouse! Having someone you trust to vent your feelings and frustrations to after a long, difficult day can significantly ease your burden while everyone is still adjusting to their new roles in this blended family.

This chapter will offer helpful advice for how to nurture a working partnership for parenting your children and step-children. Strategy #5 calls for a number of skills and a lot of patience, so... be patient. Our focus will be on clear communications, establishing realistic expectations, and establishing roles and responsibilities.

Clear Communication

As with all relationships, communication is key. Words are used to express needs, doubts, worries, concerns and accomplishments, yet many people lack good communication skills. If you have been told that you are not an adequate communicator, it is time to get some help and make some significant effort to improve. As part of a team, if each of you cannot decode the other's thoughts and sentiments, the messages to your step-children and to one another will be blurred and confusing.

There are many reasons for poor communication skills ranging from sheer laziness to an inability to prioritize thoughts and feelings, or a problem with choosing words that adequately describe those thoughts and feelings. This is not always easy for many people who have learned over years to shield their vulnerability and hide their inadequacies. However, since the method in which you choose to communicate will either enhance or take away from your goal—successful marriage and step-parenting—it is never too late to correct dysfunctional communication.

The list below points out some basic elements to clear communication. Keep in mind that you'll need to use this list with patience. We recommend that you and your partner find a time to "take this course" together. Like anything else that attempts to change old habits, it is not just the *study* of this list that is important, but the *practice* of this list. Over time, your newly learned methods of communication will come more naturally to you both, with the result worth all of the effort!

1. Make your thoughts known by using clear and concise language. In other words, do not hold back on your feelings, wishes, thoughts or expectations, and do not expect that your partner "should" be able to understand where you are coming from, if he or she does not. The very idea of making a thought clear is to find language that is easily interpreted by the receiver. For example, if you are asking, "Do you think I am fat?" do not hide it

in a sentence like "Do you like my outfit?" Say what you mean, and expect an honest answer. If you then punish your spouse for answering your question honestly, they are likely to "censor" their response next time.

2. Choose a time when your partner is more likely to be receptive to receive your message.

3. Ask your partner to repeat what they have heard you say to be certain that you have expressed your thoughts in a way that is being understood.

4. If your partner has misunderstood your message, rephrase your information in a somewhat different manner; ask for your message to be repeated back to you.

5. When a problem is being discussed, come to some mutually-agreed-upon resolution during the conversation, even if that resolution is to table the discussion until a later date, or until further information is provided.

6. Seek compromise.

7. Find eventual resolution; unresolved discussions do not go away, they escalate into arguments.

8. Do not raise your voice.

9. Do not bring other subjects or past examples into your discussion of a current problem.

10. Converse fairly. That means:

    • Don't skew the questions to reflect the answer you want to hear.

    • Don't punish the other person if you don't agree with their response to your question.

    • Remember that, in some instances, the question may have been misunderstood; in others, it simply is viewed differently than you view it.

    • Sometimes you may end up resolving a dispute by "agreeing to disagree."

    • Try not to use words such as "always" and "never," as these often elicit a defensive response. For example, if you say, "You *never* take my feelings into consideration," you will likely get a response that is equally abrupt, with little communication-resolution being exchanged.

- Another derogatory sentence-structure involves the use of the word "you," as in: "You don't come to the dinner table on time because 'you' don't care that I slaved over a hot stove all afternoon." A better approach might be: "I look forward to eating dinner with you each night and I feel hurt that I am often sitting by myself."

Appreciate Gender Differences

We must warn you, however, that for your communication to be effectively received it must be effectively given. It is no secret that men and women communicate differently; men tend to want to eliminate the story-line and cut to the chase, while women generally linger on every detail, telling the story in chronologic chapters. Men do not appreciate long, drawn-out tales. While they may not show it, somewhere during a woman's detailed version of her day's events, he may have mentally tuned her out, not because he doesn't love her, but because his attention span has reached its limit. If you are a step-*mother*, as you talk to your husband you will have to organize your news in brief, to-the-point conversation, allowing for interruptions if necessary. Keep in mind that men want to know exactly what the problem is, what they are up against, and how they are expected to "fix" a problem; men are "fixers."

On the other hand, women rarely jump head-on into a story without an introduction, a description of setting and a resume on each of the cast of characters. As a step-*father*, when you talk to your wife you may find it useful to begin at the beginning, allowing for a multitude of clarifications until the story flows.

Women like to communicate; it's one of their strong points. Men do not; it's one of their weaknesses. However, in a blended family the communication between the parent and step-parent is of paramount importance, especially while everyone is settling in with this new marriage and family structure. We consider it a necessity to plan a time, either after dinner, during an evening walk, or after the children have been put to bed, to spend at least fifteen minutes to one-half hour discussing both problems and successes in detail.

It is important that we add a disclaimer here. We are not insinuating that *all* women like to communicate in detail, nor that *all* men cannot communicate adequately. However, during our more than twenty-seven years in office practice, that seems to be the common denominator for each of the genders.

People like to know that they are heard! Just because a woman needs to express her frustrations, does not mean that she (like her male partner) is looking for immediate, specific solutions. Often, while women can figure out their own solutions to problems that arise, they still have a need to rehash the unfairness of issues or the audacity of people. For instance, if your wife is the step-mother of your children, and she delights in telling you how unappreciative your children are, then allow her to talk. If she wants you to talk to the children or make a plan to correct a situation, she will ask. Otherwise, let her talk. Many problems are resolved through talking, which by the way, is the essence of the "talking-cure."

When you communicate with your spouse—male or female—speak in clear, specific language, not in code. By "code" we mean hiding your true sentiments inside of sentences that have to be reconfigured or unearthed by the listener. By being "clear" we mean making your wishes or sentiments known without minimizing them or beating around the bush. For example, if you are frustrated, say so. Then try to attach your frustrations to a specific incident or feeling. For example, "Mary, I feel hurt when I help you around the house and you don't acknowledge my efforts." Most frustrations stem from either feeling "unappreciated" or "hurt"—those are the words you should use when trying to elicit support from your spouse.

Tony's Story

Tony came into our office at his wit's end. He said, "Every time Charmaine has a complaint about the kids I'm right there to solve the problem. I have great ideas too. Instead of thanking me, she ends up taking the anger she had with the kids and turning it onto me, when all I am trying to do is help! I don't get it!"

Charmaine was shocked and surprised to hear Tony's take on things. She said, "All I want to do is have him listen to me, but instead he thinks he knows it all! He butts into my conversations with this idea and that idea to make things better. I think he just wants to hurry up and get the conversation over with so he can go back to watching television. I'm fed up with all his unwanted advice! Right now I could use a lot more sympathy and a lot less control!"

As in Tony's case, it is not surprising that most husbands will throw their hands in the air when their best efforts fail to get them points with their wives. It is not so much that they are opposed to addressing issues; after all, they know that being a step-mother is often as thankless a job as being a biologic mother, but they are opposed to addressing issues for which they are then reprimanded. In other words, if, as a step-mother, you solicit your husband to step in and speak to the children on your behalf, and then mid-way through his intervention you chastise him for being too strict, you have not only undermined him in front of his children, but you have also sabotaged your own chances of getting him to volunteer for the position the next time.

Realistic Expectations

You and your spouse have a wonderful opportunity to really make a difference in the lives of the children with whom you have been entrusted. That can only occur when all the individual members come together as a team, working with each other's strengths and weaknesses, supporting each other with compassion, humor and understanding, and cheering each other on as you cross the finish line to success.

When families blend, there are so many variables to work with:

- You might have come from a large family with many siblings, and have a high tolerance for the unexpected turmoil that can erupt with children at any time. Your spouse may have come from a small family of obedient, disciplined, reserved children who rarely if ever spoke out of turn.
- You might have difficulty expressing your feelings, while your spouse speaks every thought that he or she has.
- One of you might react immediately to a request for information, while the other may be used to digesting information slowly and processing commentary over hours or even days.

In other words, it will be easier for one of you to progress through the "blending" period less scathed than the other.

Then, there are almost always the unconscious expectations of the children toward blending. Usually these are unrealistically positive, leading to disappointment and disillusionment fairly rapidly. Understandably then, it is nearly impossible to anticipate outcomes of events, or how various members will react. Yet, so many parent-partners do just that. Whether the biologic parent is male or female, they often unrealistically assume that not only will their children be thrilled with the prospect of a new step-parent, but that the step-parent will be bubbling over with joy at the opportunity to put all of their needs on the back burner to raise children. This might eventually come to pass ... but certainly it is unlikely in the first year of adjustment.

You and your spouse should work out what your expectations are with regard to rectifying a problem with the step-children *before* you call them in for a family meeting. If you simply want your spouse to reiterate your directives, let them know that. If you need him or her to step in and be assertive, let them know that as well. However, don't forget that, during the first few months of step-parenting, it is best that the biologic parent run any family meetings and issue directives. Not until the first year approaches will your step-children be more receptive to you as an integral member of the family, and not just an individual who makes rules and creates problems. If your spouse does not back you on any of your concerns or complaints privately, it is certainly unlikely that his or her lack of support can do anything but point a finger at you as the "troublemaker."

To help you pinpoint exactly where preconceived notions might clash (or did clash) with unreasonable expectations, we offer your parenting team the following list of questions to consider together. Ask each other to identify some possible sources of friction in your own family, and do your best to answer truthfully.

Problems / Questions To Consider

You will find it easier to anticipate speed bumps in the road of step-parenting when these are flagged ahead of time—that is, identified specifically, and on a personal level. We have listed several "fill in the blank" sentences to give you pause for thought. If you are truly honest with your feelings as you respond to these fragmented sentences, you might gain valuable insight into your expectations, realistic or not. This sentence completion exercise is especially valuable if your spouse completes it as well. Then, as the two of you share your expectations, it not only opens the lines of communication, but allows each of you a glimpse into the underpinnings of potential problems before they arise.

This exercise should be completed within one or two sittings; after that, let the questions "rest." You can go back to finish or further develop your responses at another time, as you feel inclined. You might be surprised to learn just how reasonable, or unreasonable, your expectations are.

1. I was tired of being a single parent so I looked for a partner who would …
2. I imagined that my time would be freed up once I married and I could …
3. I expect a man to do …
4. I expect a woman to do …
5. If things are not running smoothly I feel that my partner should handle the children because …
6. I feel that I work harder than my partner and therefore …
7. I feel that my partner doesn't appreciate me and so I …
8. Secretly I am disappointed in the allocation of my responsibilities with the children; it would be fairer if …
9. I do (do not) believe things would get easier if …
10. I think we got off on the wrong foot when …
11. I am still upset when I was blamed for …

The story of Kate and Will that follows dynamically illustrates the preconceived notions that come with illusory thinking.

Kate's Story

When Kate and Will arrived in our office, Will's body language more than his words, distanced him from his wife of three months. He recounted how the marriage had changed *her*; how the tension in the household was a deterrent to the harmonious family that he and his two children (ages eight and eleven) had before Kate moved in. As he described the negative mood that hung over his home, his eyes shifted to

Kate, who remained docile and passive until their third session. At that meeting she found her voice, and was eager to turn back the clock to the time when the relationship had progressed from casual dating to talks of marriage.

Kate had never had children of her own, although she wanted children very badly. When she fell in love with Will, his enthusiasm about his children was contagious, and both of them dreamed of becoming a family. Will had big plans for his girls, and even bigger plans for Kate. He pictured her teaching the children everything they needed to know about "girl stuff." He imagined her fussing with their hair, selecting their clothing, teaching them to cook, and having late talks into the night. While Kate was dreaming about her wedding day, Will was dreaming about her taking some of the responsibility of child-rearing off his hands.

Kate was immediately taken with the good natured girls; they were friendly and open, anxious to include her in their school work and plans for the summer. That was, until they realized that she was not merely a fun companion, but that their father was planning to marry her. She would be their step-mother! That is when everything changed. The girls' attitudes became sullen and defiant; they locked themselves in their bedrooms and refused to carry on conversations at the dinner table. When Kate entered a room, they exited.

Will was shocked at his children's behavior and pressed Kate for answers. He wanted to know why his children were acting that way, and what Kate was doing wrong. He then said, "Why can't you try to be more like their biologic mother is, so they will feel more comfortable with you?" Kate was speechless, but her tears spoke volumes.

In an individual session Will was openly angry at Kate. He was so busy blaming her for the household disharmony that he failed to recognize his own responsibility for the turmoil he created. If he had owned up to his urgency to be married and the picture-perfect family he painted in his mind, he might have recognized that he was setting everyone up for failure. Also, if the children had more time to become acquainted with Kate before their father announced wedding plans, the positive experiences they had been sharing would have bolstered their mutual affection. Instead, the children felt blind-sided and acted out with anger and confusion. It was not Kate that they were angry at, but their father whom they believed betrayed them by posing Kate as "just a friend," placing them in a precarious position with their biologic mother.

Will's children soon voiced their anger at his lack of honesty, and their concern that he would lavish all of his affection on Kate, leaving none for them. Will found it difficult to get in touch with his unconscious agenda in his decision to marry Kate. Once he gained insight, however, he realized that he wanted to secure Kate not only as a wife, but as a step-mother so that he could leave the parenting to someone else. He truly loved his daughters, but he believed himself inadequate to father girls without a woman close at hand.

Will admitted that his poor choices and impulsive actions had positioned Kate as a scapegoat for the children's acting out. The children admitted they really loved Kate, sharing that their fear of losing their father is what motivated them to try to push her away. Kate was willing to try again, once Will affirmed that he really did love her with all his heart.

It was a long first year, but they made it! When we last saw them, year two was looking so much brighter! Clearly, reaching deeper into unconscious motivations allowed both Will and Kate to weed out "neediness" from a true desire to share their lives together. They could do this based upon their belief that not *only* love, but *real partnering*, could help them attain their goals.

Emotional Management

Many new step-parents complain that their spouse doesn't support them during boundary-making or discipline. That lack of support may have more to do with the step-parent's energy surrounding the issue, rather than a disagreement with the issue itself. Sometimes a step-parent mistakenly believes that, regardless of how petty an incident, or how unfavorably a conflict turned out, the biologic parent must clearly "choose sides"—either the children's or theirs—creating a sort of sibling-rivalry situation. We are big fans of unity among the parents, but if there is a tendency for you, as a step-parent, to react on emotional impulse, we must agree that it is unreasonable to expect your spouse to jump onto an out-of-control train.

Often a new step-mother will come to the office complaining that her husband never supports her when she is angry at her step-children. With a little deeper exploration, however, those same new step-parents admit to being out of control with their anger or demands.

Believe it or not, however, it is often the step-parent who is the more emotionally stable individual when it comes to making logical decisions, and the biologic parent who feels "betrayed" because their anger has blinded their objectivity. A spouse who has recently divorced may still harbor a lot of anger aimed at the former spouse, but this anger may be displaced onto the current spouse. In a two-parent biological marriage, when one natural parent is unable or unwilling to take control of a particular situation, the other steps in; in other words they play off each other's strengths. In a blended family however, when the weaker parent happens to be the biologic parent, this often forces the step-parent to substitute for the stronger parent, and has negative ramifications, involving acts of rebellion and opposition by the step-children.

Rachael's Story

Rachael begged her mother for an appointment with a therapist so that she could explain her "miserable" living conditions. By any standard, Rachael's home and neighborhood were lovely; her mother was loving and caring, and she had many friends. The only change that precipitated her "misery" was the addition of her step-father, Bill. She accused him of trying to ruin her life by not allowing her to use her cell phone after ten o'clock or do her homework in front of the television set like her father does. He also "ruined her life" by not allowing her to use the Internet unless she was in an open room.

We were quite impressed by Rachael's Academy-Award-winning act to which her mother, so blinded by her emotional attachment to her daughter, was only too happy to give her a standing ovation. We spent some time with the mother in individual sessions and explained that although her daughter felt confined, her husband was using sound, caring, and well-thought-out advice to protect his step-daughter from sexual predators and other unseemly characters. He was also concerned about her lack of sleep and poor grades in school. As her mother began to form a more healthy relationship with her daughter, she began working as a team with Rachael's step-father in setting boundaries and issuing consequences when those boundaries were disregarded. After two months of parenting in a united manner, Rachael began to understand what her role in the family was, and where she was located on the Family Hierarchy Ladder. Her mother reported to us that Bill was finally being given the respect from his step-daughter that he deserved.

Children are much more likely to point a finger at a "mean step-parent" than a biologic parent who expects the same reasonable behavior; this places the step-parent in the precarious position of being the target of resentment, anger and hostility.

In any case, there should be no reason to stoop to screaming, crying, or walking out of the house during a disagreement with your step-children (or your biologic children for that matter). If such things do happen, however, the "screamer" has no grounds to expect his or her spouse to follow close behind. If you feel you must resort to screaming, please save it for something that warrants a tiny bit of irrationality—such as when your step-child steals the family car, or charges clothing on your credit card without permission. Otherwise, as the adult, it is necessary to control your impulses, circle the wagons, and unify your efforts with your partner to support each other.

Remember, there will be disagreements between parents, but these should be kept private and personal. You and your spouse owe it to yourselves and your children to keep your voices controlled, to be mindful that the content of your dissatisfaction with each other should be fair, and your problem-related conversations out of earshot of the children. If something is occurring that needs to be attended to immediately, and there are children present, it is always a good idea to have worked out a code word, such as "UNCLE," to denote an adult "time out" and a quick meeting in another room to resolve the issue. As always, we strive for excellence in step-parenting by team parenting!

Stephen's Story

Stephen couldn't believe that in the six short months he had married into Ruthie's family he had become the brunt of so many arguments. Ruthie's two children—Todd, age four, and Susie, age seven—had shown him almost no respect. He came into the office stating, "I didn't take this kind of 'mouthiness' from my own kids, and I am certainly not going to take it from somebody else's."

That he had distinguished his step-children as "somebody else's" kids was not going to gain him any popularity or loyalty from his step-children. Nonetheless, Ruthie had a responsibility, which she didn't take, to insure that her children were taught to respect their elders—in this case, Stephen. Because she didn't step in to correct them when they spoke rudely to him, they took it to mean that their mother was aligning herself with them. At this point we had to agree with them, as this *was* the message she was giving. Unconsciously, the real reason that Ruthie was siding with her children stemmed from her own frustration and anger at Stephen. She said, "He wasn't in the house one week before he started issuing orders like the kids were in the military." Within days her children were upset, and within weeks they were in full-fledged revolt against him.

Prior to Stephen, Ruthie had been married to a man who had similar traits to herself; both were without plans or rules, and both allowed the children free rein in the house. Rather than matching up their parenting philosophies prior to their marriage, Ruthie and Stephen just assumed that somehow it would all work itself out. As they sat in our office with their arms tightly crossed, it was clear that it would not.

Stephen's personality was dictatorial while Ruthie was whimsical and expressive. Ruthie felt bulldozed by her husband's strong personality and wanted to protect her children from his demands. However, without confronting him, she was giving a mixed message to her children and no message to Stephen. At first, Stephen felt as though even we were "ganging up" on him, or at least conspiring with Ruthie. But before long, he realized that by demanding obedience and respect from children, you are likely to receive just the opposite.

They both worked on their communication skills with each other, as well as on compromising some of their expectations. We helped Stephen to appreciate the Family Hierarchy

Ladder and the need to pace himself until he was firmly established with his step-children as a member of the family. We explained that there was no need for him to "take over" his step-children, but rather to learn by observation their interactions and idiosyncrasies. Later, he and his wife could co-parent by highlighting those issues that needed to be fine-tuned.

Because Stephen and Ruthie agreed to hone in on their communication methods and express their feelings clearly and openly, there should be a happy ending to both the marriage and Stephen's step-parenting endeavors.

Stephen and Ruthie discovered that children of every age expect to be parented, although they like to rebel against anyone in authority whom they perceive interferes with their premature desire for total autonomy. Ruthie needed to learn that children are neither mature nor wise enough to govern their own behavior; if they were, there would be no need for parents. She now understands that children require a structured set of values and principles, established by their parent and step-parent, to which they must adhere. If those boundaries are not enforced, not only will the children learn to disrespect authority, but each partner in this "team" will learn to disrespect the other. (See Strategy #3 for a treatment of Boundaries and Consequences.)

Defining Roles and Responsibilities

In a traditional marriage the husband was expected to go to work and bring home the money, or simply put, to hunt and gather, while the wife's role was defined as a homemaker and mother. Times have changed, and there are now many options in how your roles are defined. Some men stay home with the kids while the wives go to work. Other men and women share the workload equally. Some women believe it is their job to "do it all," including working outside the home, contributing to the family budget, rearing the children or step-children, and taking all the responsibility of cooking and cleaning. Some men still feel emasculated if they pitch in with childcare, and "controlled" if they do not make and enforce all the rules and dictate all the schedules. Fortunately, such men are now the exceptions, no longer the rule. Most twenty-first-century men recognize and encourage the value of true partnering, and have reaped the benefits of a closer, more bonded family because of it.

Regardless of how you and your parent-partner decide to set up house and assign the various child-care responsibilities, this should be mutually agreed upon and fair to each of you. For example, one of you might be exceptionally talented in the kitchen, while the other has strengths in home repair. By making a list of all chores and responsibilities that it takes to make up your particular household, each of you will be more aware of the enormity of the responsibilities that should not fall unfairly—unevenly—upon one person's shoulders. Most of these responsibilities can be tackled together so much more efficiently than tackled alone.

Here is a short list of some items that need to be dealt with in every family. Please add those individual items that apply uniquely to your own blended family.

1. Carpooling
2. Making breakfast for the children before school
3. Cleaning the house
4. Yard work
5. Grocery shopping
6. Car maintenance
7. Laundry
8. Homework
9. Dinner preparation
10. Scheduling doctor and dentist visits

By actually writing down each and every responsibility to be addressed, you help to eliminate the guesswork about what things have to be accomplished. The old saying "Knowledge is Power" holds true when it comes to delegating and sharing. Traditional households have given way to two-parent working households where often both adults are exhausted and their roles at home are blurred and ill-defined. Without discussing and resolving your responsibilities, resentment can build up quickly and the children (or your marriage) will soon suffer the fallout.

Susan's Story

Susan was fed up enough to make an appointment for she and her husband Pete to begin therapy. She explained that early in their marriage she had taken all the responsibility for childcare of her step-children because Pete seemed completely inadequate to assume a responsible parenting role. Pete said it was never his job to raise the children during his first marriage, and after his wife died, he wasted no time finding a "replacement."

Susan didn't mind caring for her step-children, whom she grew to love very much, but she was completely stressed by the amount of responsibility that found its way to her side of the column, while Pete's responsibilities dwindled. On their second anniversary, Susan evaluated her situation; by that time she had become a step-mother, full-time career woman, housekeeper, cook, nurse, and chauffeur. Pete on the other hand came home from work only after he stopped at the local bar and had a few beers with his buddies, most of whom were single. Then he grabbed his dinner plate, sat down on the couch, and settled in for the night in front of the television set. When he had finally had enough of television, he made his way into the bedroom for sex.

It was clear that Pete had gotten away with his irresponsible attitude in his first marriage and mimicked this behavior in his second marriage. He told us what he knew we *wanted to hear*, but did little about changing his behavior until Susan filed for divorce. Pete didn't want to lose Susan and also didn't want his children to become victims of a second splintered marriage. By default, he began earnestly working on his marriage, and his slow march toward adulthood.

Life's Little Extras

Pete and Susan's story demonstrates how an unfair burden of major responsibilities can bode badly in marriage. Aside from our short list of everyday responsibilities that need to be dealt with in your family, there will always be those "extras," which will crop up daily. When these minute-to-minute tasks are not clearly considered, one spouse may infer that the other has it "easy" in comparison. Nothing puts a damper on a marital relationship faster than this kind of comparing.

Consider your family's important "little extras." Add them to your list of general responsibilities. Here are a few of our suggestions to help get you started. Who will:
1. Bake cupcakes for children's school birthdays?
2. Go to the library to get ideas for the science projects?
3. Buy or help create the Halloween costumes, and buy the candy for trick or treaters?
4. Get the piano tuned in time for piano lessons?
5. Take the children to band practice, baseball tryouts, scout meetings?
6. Get the washing machine repaired?
7. Call the pest control service to report ants in the kitchen?

8. Weed the garden?
9. Take the children out for pizza for a good report card?
10. Schedule the "date night" for husband and wife alone?

Keep Laughing

Probably the most important thing to remember is not on the list above, but should be employed as much as possible. That is to keep your sense of humor. When the toilet overflows, your favorite platter shatters into a million pieces, and great grandpa's bottle of 100-year-old wine is accidentally opened, you might as well look for the silver lining in the otherwise sky full of clouds. All of this will pass ... it always does ... and what you want to wind up with is each other, and a whole bunch of hilarious memories!

Child Support

The responsibility of one or both of you to pay child support sometimes becomes an issue in your current marriage for several reasons, the least of which is that it may become a financial burden in the budget. Unfortunately, until child support is no longer an issue, rather than complaining about the monthly financial strain, both of you should put your heads together to find some resolution, and ask a few simple questions, to ensure there are no unresolved or hidden animosities around money. Question, for example, "Is the money that is used toward child support really straining the budget?" If so, "Can the budget be modified?" "Is the individual whose responsibility it is to pay child support payments doing this on time, or are they remiss in this obligation, thereby putting the burden on the other spouse to oversee this obligation?" "Does the parent who is responsible for paying the child support believe that the support is in fact being spent carelessly by the former spouse, and not on the children?" "Have circumstances changed—such as wage loss or job termination—and should there be a modification of child support?"

Again, communication is key so that resentment does not build. Often, where child support issues are concerned, this is a time where allowing your partner to vent his or her feelings is more important than actually coming up with a solution to a problem that cannot immediately be solved. Remember, if this topic becomes a major source of angst refer to Strategy #8, Get the Help You Need.

Helping Each Other Over the Rough Spots

Working as a team, doing the right thing, setting your needs aside, and blending parenting-philosophies is a high-level aim. It requires the knowledge of reasonable childhood behavior throughout their developmental stages, mutual respect and admiration for the skills that your partner possesses, and a true desire to continue perfecting those parenting skills. Not everyone is equipped with these necessary skills. If you or your partner could use some assistance, seek help through reading, therapy, or parenting classes. See Strategy #8, which includes our Resource Guide. Remember, if you or your spouse parent inadequately, your step-children will ultimately suffer. The bottom line is this: You have a right to expect to be emotionally supported by your spouse. If you are good enough to contribute financially to the marriage and responsible enough to take on the job of step-parenting, then we believe you have earned the right to be respected in your household. Self-respect comes with a price … what's yours?

Guilt left over from divorce, and guilt at previously poor parenting, is often the single-most identified culprit standing between a parent applying proper expectations and one who pretends not to notice undisciplined children. If your guilt is paralyzing you or clouding your judgment, you surely cannot expect your parent-partner to stand by helplessly as you allow yourself to be trampled by your children, or worse, allow your children to trample your parent-partner. This is where parent-partners can *really help each other* by identifying and alleviating unnecessary guilt and the corresponding fear that your children or step-children will not love you if you do not give in to all their demands.

The fact that your children or step-children may have suffered through a miserable divorce is unfortunate, but it does not give them a free pass to run amuck. That a child comes from a divorced family may be a fact, but that does not dictate that their lives cannot be happy, productive and loving even though their parents reside in two separate households.

Children expect to have rules, and they expect you to enforce those rules if you really love them. They will kick and scream every step of the way, but there is something very comforting to them in finding that their parent-partners are willing to take the harder road. When parents, often aided by their parent-partners, do the right thing, the children learn that although the original marriage no longer exists, their family does.

❖

You have come this far, and with the information you have gained and the storms you have weathered together you can go anywhere from here! Before you know it the children will be all grown, and you and your spouse will have the rest of your lives to look over your handiwork and know that your sacrifices have made all the difference.

STRATEGY #6
Respect the Past As You Create the Future
Blend New and Old Memories

This chapter is about new beginnings: about affirming new bonds, creating a new life together, planning ahead, and carving out new pathways for your blended family. At the same time, this chapter is about honoring the past. Your step-children have a history ... grandparents, traditions, and memories; it is these memories that invoke nostalgia, and are the building blocks for the further foundation of personality-shaping and ego-strength.

The times when you and your step-children skipped flat stones across a babbling brook, or shaped cookie dough into twisted pretzels to be baked and salted, are often as important as expensive trips to Disney World, or purchasing a teenager's first car.

Think back to your own childhood and you will likely recall events with relatives that were seemingly based upon nothing more than eating around a holiday table. Yet, these memories mean more than almost any material possession you have acquired. Your step-children have those same memories, as well as memories which they will share with you, to recall lovingly later in life.

Adults are also not the only ones who carry around emotional suitcases; children have their fair share of luggage weighed down with "emotional stuff." You may have purged some of your issues, thereby lightening your load, but children have a more difficult time "letting go." Old memories cannot be swept under the rug or discarded in tomorrow's trash pickup.

There is a process to bridging gaps, and as in everything else it is a two part deal. First you must know what you're up against, and second you must use a combination of patience and timing for the best results. With this in mind, Strategy # 6—blending new and old—will be applied to three important issues:

Part I: Blending traditions
Part II: Determining where to live, and
Part III: Honoring our extended families.

PART I: Blending Traditions

Some concepts are so steeped in tradition that they are rarely analyzed. Religion, holidays, family recipes, reunions, Alma-Maters ... are all among those things held dear from generation to generation within a family. Not surprisingly, when one family steeped in one set of traditions begins to blend with an entirely different set of traditions held fast by another family, there are obstacles to overcome while learning to embrace foreign philosophies.

Differences in family traditions, and the confusion that may be caused to children who are suddenly thrust into a new set of rituals, are subjects that come up regularly when blending families. As we explain to our patients, there is room enough for *all* points of view and customs. What better way to educate and expose children to the vastness of individuality than to allow them to experience first-hand the meaning of Christmas, Chanukah, Divali or Ramadan; the similarities between confession and Yom Kippur; the celebration of confirmation and Bar or Bat Mitzvahs.

Religious Differences

If we are to espouse the idea that children cannot assimilate the distinctness of two separate religious views, then how are we to believe it is acceptable to expose them to two different languages? What's more, how could we successfully teach two languages to toddlers who are barely able to speak? People underestimate children—they always have and always will. Children are not fragile little people who cannot juggle multiple thoughts and opinions; rather they are cerebral young people who can incorporate differences in people with more acceptance and tolerance than most adults. For the most part, it is the adults who cannot see past their blinders, while children find great adventure and joy in learning and participating in the cultures and traditions of others. Often, in blended families, one adult will be expected to acquiesce to the other, especially when religious convictions are at stake. This practice not only deprives that adult of his or her rightful cultural heritage, but it denies children the broader scope of exposure. Some organized religions refuse to marry couples of different faiths unless one "gives up" their faith and promises to raise the children in the other. Individually and as a couple, you certainly have the right to abandon your faith if that is what you choose, but you should not be manipulated to obliterate generations of belief to please an institution.

If you have promised to raise your step-children in a certain faith, then do so, but not at the cost of keeping your traditions cloaked in darkness. Allow your step-children to share in your religious customs as well, especially if these are celebrated among members of your extended family. In our opinion it is time for people to break loose of the religious and racial constraints and have a look around. We are all striving for peace and harmony, and the fastest way to reach it is to bring your neighbor along.

Holiday Rituals

Some families celebrate the opening of gifts on Christmas Eve rather than Christmas morning. Some religious or ethnic groups consider Halloween to be sacrilegious, while others see it as nothing more than a time to let loose and put on some costumes for trick or treat. There are as many variables in holiday rituals as there are individuals who celebrate them. Whether there is a turkey or a dumpling soup on a holiday table; whether there is pickled fish or colored eggs, a birthday cake or mango rice, we are all simply honoring the memories of our ancestors and paying homage in the way we have been taught. Continue your celebrations, teaching your step-children that there is room for all races, all ethnicities, all religions and all individuals. On a personal note, we believe that by eliminating separatism, we would all be one step closer to world peace.

Family Memorabilia

Making new memories and keeping old ones includes organizing family photos so that every important member of the family, blended or natural, is represented. As a step-parent you might feel saddened or even threatened to find that your step-children insist that their absent biologic parent's photo still has the place of honor above the mantle. While this prominent location might have to be negotiated, what is vital is that your step-children believe that no one is trying to "erase" their other biologic parent. Because they often need visual reassurance that the other parent still exists in their new household, it is a wise step-parent who agrees to leave the parent's picture on the wall, or displayed on the photo table.

This, of course, goes right to the heart of your feelings of security or insecurity. If you are able to depersonalize these feelings and take yourself out of the equation you will be serving your children. Their desire to have a visual reminder of their parent while that parent is not physically present is not a slur to you, but a real longing to connect to something they have lost. They are doing the best they can with so many upheavals—a splintered family, a new step-parent, new blended step-siblings and new housing. Think of these photographs as security blankets, not meant to be kept forever, but just for the times when a little comfort goes a long way.

Rhonda's Story

Sally and Sarah were products of divorce. When both were in middle school their parents separated and after two long years of arguing, the divorce was final. One year later their father married Rhonda, and their mother moved off to Idaho to live with a bohemian ski instructor who didn't like children. It was decided that the girls would live with their father and Rhonda. Still reeling from the loss of their family unit as well as the departure of their mother who now lived more than nine-hundred miles away, they returned home from visiting Idaho for a two-week Spring break to find a completely renovated bedroom. The little picture window that looked out onto a great oak tree had been turned into Bahamian-style window shutters. In fact, the entire once-Victorian room with lace curtains and flowered wallpaper had been transformed into a scene from a tropical photo shoot. Life-sized faux banana trees stood where the antique coat-rack had displayed their vintage hats; orange, lime green and bright yellow adorned the walls in shocking hues.

Rhonda couldn't wait to see their expressions as the girls opened the door to their bedroom, but what she witnessed was not the expression she had hoped. Within minutes they were both crying and yelling, telling her she had no right to meddle into their things, especially the lace curtains, which were not only gone but had been hauled away. "But the curtains were yellowed and frayed," Rhonda said defensively, saddened by what she believed was a complete lack of appreciation for what she had done. The response from the girls said everything, "They may have been frayed, but they were all we had left of Mom. She made them for us."

Items considered special to one person are often discarded by another. Often it is not the actual material item, but the memories associated with the person who gave the item, or the circumstances in which the item came to be, that gives it such a place of reverence. In the enthusiasm to be the perfect step-parent, you might be tempted to replace an old leather baseball glove with a brand new one, or discard the worn, threadbare comforter with a more updated quilt. But, in your desire to make things better, you may in fact be inadvertently discarding a treasured possession.

Mistakes in this domain are bound to happen: no one could be held responsible for tossing out scraps of material, only to find out that these were once promised by a now deceased parent to be made into a memory quilt. If you have made the mistake of tidying up clutter only to throw away sentimental items, retrieve them if you can, and truly apologize if you cannot. Your step-child will forgive a blunder that was made from a sincere desire to help, but they will not easily forgive blunders that continue out of insensitivity.

Each person needs their "space" and their "stuff." It might be best to help your step-children pack some of their "stuff" away in water-tight containers to be stored in the attic. When you retrieve them later, like when they graduate from college or celebrate the birth of their child, don't be surprised if they look at you as if you have two heads, when you proudly display how carefully you stored their prized possessions. Only then you will have their blessings to throw such things out!

The Other Parent's Holidays

This is a good place to offer some advice about holiday celebrations that involve the other biologic parent. When the other parent's birthday is coming up, or Mother's Day, or Father's Day and your step-children don't have spending money or the ability to drive to a store, it is kind of you to assist them in not only remembering the occasion, but helping them make or purchase an appropriate gift or card. You may have lots of dissention to this idea among your friends and associates, but kindness cannot be measured except in the ripple effect that continues throughout your relationship with your step-children. It's the right thing to do.

Each individual has a "favorite" holiday, and may tend to go overboard (from someone else's perspective) in decorating, cooking and perhaps even gift-giving. If birthday celebrations are really your "thing"—maybe you bake a birthday cake like no one else can—why not really extend yourself and ask your children if they would like to invite the other biologic parent to a "surprise" birthday party at your house. You and your current spouse might engage the children in putting up crepe-paper streamers, blowing up balloons, and setting the birthday table. Your step-children will likely have good ideas about the birthday menu, recalling the other parent's favorite foods. This act of simple kindness will go a long way in teaching lessons on forgiveness, civility, family, and the true blending of families.

Even within your own family structure, you and your spouse may have special traditions that can be shared. For instance, if your spouse just loves dressing up in Halloween costumes and trick or treating, go along with it, get your step-children involved, and come up with a "theme" you can all participate in. It may seem lame to be such overgrown ghosts or goblins ringing doorbells for penny candy but the memories to be shared will be priceless!

Weddings—Plans and Protocol

Wedding plans are a wonderful part of being in love, but when your wedding is also the beginning of a blended family, more than just your individual preferences will have to share center stage. Depending on your situation, your wedding plans may have been discussed during a long engagement period, during which time the children have had time to adjust to the idea of their parent no longer being available for the "fantasy" return to the prior parent. However, given twenty-first-century impulsivity, more and more adults are caught up in a whirlwind romance and quickie wedding. This doesn't give the kids much time to process changes that are not only occurring to you as the adult, but to them.

If there was a perfectly scripted engagement, it would be the proposing adult "clearing" the decision to pop the question with the children from one or both sides of the biologic lines. With your step-children's enthusiasm and excitement to be a part of such a big decision, many of them will find themselves rooting for both of you, regardless of their dashed dreams of reuniting their parents. Then, once the recipient of the proposal agrees to be married, everyone shares in the moment. This will be their first memory marking the beginning of their blended family.

If there is to be a traditional wedding, it is likely that your children from your former marriage, as well as your new step-children will attend, if not actively participate. This is where, as a step-parent, you will have to be skilled in fairness, or at least the perception of fairness. Your daughter, for example, cannot be a flower girl if your husband's daughter is seated in the first pew as an onlooker. His grown son cannot be best man, if your grown son is merely escorting guests to their seats. Everyone is going to have to be made to feel special, or no one should participate in the actual wedding ceremony.

At the reception, either every child is seated at the head table or none of the children is seated there. If the children are seated at other tables, do you want to mix both families, or keep them separate? There is no correct answer, other than to know that generally younger children will expect to have some special task in the nuptials, whereas teens are often just as happy to perhaps make the centerpieces and sit out the rest.

You and your spouse are the best judges of who should do what with whom, but be aware that you are marrying each other's *entire family*, and therefore sharing the day with them.

If your young step-children are invited to be a part of the wedding party, decisions have to be made as to who will dress them. If that individual is their biological parent, and in this case, not the parent you are marrying, then are you going to invite that parent to the wedding as well? Several decades ago that statement would not only be ridiculous, but shocking. However in today's "anything goes" culture, many couples do invite their former spouses, especially if their biologic children are going to need assistance either before, during, or after the actual ceremony and well into the reception.

Regardless of how the special titles are divided, each child from both families should be introduced and acknowledged publicly by name. If the husband of the bride dances with his daughters, he should also dance with yours. If you dance with your sons, you should also dance with his. The word "fairness" cannot be highlighted enough, and unfortunately there are no wedding "do-overs." If someone has been slighted accidentally, you cannot make this event up to them.

Unfortunately, there are some biologic parents who are not supportive of their spouse's nuptials, and therefore make it difficult for the biologic children to attend the wedding without feeling an overwhelming sense of disloyalty. That is very difficult for the marital couple, but even more difficult for the children. If an older step-child makes a decision not to attend the wedding out of respect for his other biologic parent, there is little that can be done other than to let them know they will be missed. There is no need to try to make them feel badly; they already feel as bad as they ever will. Younger children should not be placed in the middle of an argument between their biologic parents over an upcoming wedding ceremony. This is just too much stress to place upon them, and frankly, these issues among former spouses should have been resolved a long time ago. They can still be resolved in months to come, but your wedding day is not the time to dredge up animosities.

Jill's Story

Jill certainly could have acted more maturely when her former husband remarried. Unfortunately her self-centered decisions impacted the children negatively.

Jill wanted no part of the news about Randolph's impending wedding; in fact she was still openly bitter about their divorce. When she found out that he asked their two children to be the ring bearer and flower girl, she was adamant that not only would they be forbidden to participate in the ceremony, they would be banned from the wedding all together. Jill raged into our office spewing obscenities about the woman Randolph was marrying, furious that her children were expected to have anything to do with their father and "the other woman."

Randolph argued that he had as much right to have the children attend his wedding as she had in refusing to allow them to attend. The battle escalated for an hour before Jill finally agreed to allow them to participate "as long as their new step-mother had nothing to do with dressing them or otherwise showing them public affection at the wedding." It was agreed. Sadly, just before the ceremony, Jill told the children how disappointed she was with them for wanting to be a part of their father's wedding after "what he did to her." The children, ages five and six, almost didn't walk down the aisle; however, they performed admirably, but their red-rimmed eyes gave away their feelings of guilt and disloyalty.

Seating Arrangements

The guest list at your wedding may be another source of contention, especially if some of the invites were friends of the former couple, and not yet friends with you. Some old friends will of course decline out of respect to the other biologic parent, but some will attend out of respect to you and your spouse. With such a mixture of guests, it is nearly impossible to decide who should be seated next to whom. In such a case a buffet style dinner may work to your advantage, as the guests can pair up with suitable dinner companions. Although buffet settings tend to make the reception take on a more informal feel, it also prevents angry or hurt feelings among the guests. If you are determined to have a formal seating chart, you should recognize those guests who are attending out of respect to one of you, but not both of you; a long-time friend of both former spouses, for example, would probably be uncomfortable seated next to the new spouse's family members.

While you're sorting out the seating arrangements and being gracious toward the former spouse, you don't want to lose sight of what is really important during this one moment in time; you are getting married! This is your time to shine. Do the best you can to smooth out any rough edges and then leave any unresolved issues for another day. You fell in love with someone who fell in love with you. What a glorious thing to have happen! Together you will carve out a new path with your blended family. We wish you nothing but happiness!

New Memories

By now you can see that there is no need to exclusively live in the past; you are not competing against old memories, you are simply adding new ones. Now is the time to make memories with your step-children: take pictures, make scrapbooks, be adventurous, explore new vacation hideaways and think about establishing yearly family reunions early. Children love to ham it up for the camera, so why not bring your camera along everywhere you go? The more pictures you snap the sooner your blended family scrapbook collection will be at the top of the pile! It won't be long before your step-children graduate high school and move away to college; from there, it is likely that they may never again reside underneath your roof.

One point of contention in a blended family is the amount of time spent as a family unit versus the amount of individual time either parent or step-parent spends alone with their bio-logic children, or the amount of time the other biologic parent spends with their children. There are some times when your step-children would like to spend some "alone" time with their biologic parent. To some of you, this may feel like a personal affront, but it really isn't. It is simply a desire to connect one-on-one with their parent. In the same way that you long for alone time with your spouse, your step-children have those same longings. Think of it this way; you and your spouse can book a cruise or a long weekend away to rekindle the bond between you, but children must be satisfied with that which they are given.

If you encourage your step-children and their parent to spend a fun evening or weekend together, or plan an activity that is special *just for them*, you will score high points in every-one's book for being so unselfish. You will certainly score high points with us for being so mature.

There are so many ways to incorporate your blended family members into one unit. Try planning a movie night once a week, with a rental movie and popcorn. Of course the dinner table is always an opportunity to bring each family member closer. Don't use this time to go over unpleasant conversation such as grades, homework or chores, but rather make it a fun time to laugh and loosen up. Perhaps you can even give a small prize each week for the person who can tell the funniest story, or the one who recalls their most embarrassing moment, with everyone voting in a secret ballot.

If you can think creatively, you have won half the battle of open, easy communication; it won't be long before each of your step-children is vying for time to giggle their way through tall tales. There will come a day when, unsolicited, your step-children make you a sweet card or gift from their heart, and it will all be worth it!

Bonding takes place in families who share time together! Bonding starts with those intangible and tangible moments that are unique only to those who are physically present during that particular time or for that particular event. As those moments begin to accumulate, they gather momentum, and soon abstract into emotions and feelings with attached memories. In this way they deepen relationship, that is, establish a "bond," between the participants. For example, suppose you take your step-children fishing every Saturday morning, and during that time, you play word association games while you wait patiently for a bite. In the end, it will not be the amount of fish you bring home, but the sense that you are trustworthy, willing to extend yourself and take time to listen and help that will bond you to your child. These memories of good times—and the high-quality relationship they reflected—will resurface even years later when your step-child, now an adult, takes his children fishing on a Saturday morning, and introduces them to (you guessed it!) word games to pass the time. These bonding experiences and the memories associated with them can continue on, in one form or other, to many loved ones who are yet to come into existence.

PART II: Housing Arrangements

Interestingly, the question "Where will we live?" is uttered by every child whose parents face divorce. It is also one of the first questions children ask when they learn they are about to be part of a blended family. If children had their way—which they do not, because you will remember the Family Hierarchy Ladder where the children have been taught that their family is not run as a democracy—you would find yourself living in six or eight different neighborhoods as they change their minds according to where their current friends live. That said, the place where you decide to live will be well thought out in terms of your financial ability, the location of your employment, the school districts, and the safety of the neighborhood.

John's Story

John, the biologic parent, and Cindy, the step-mother, spent weeks rehearsing how they would explain to their blended family (three elementary- and pre-school-age children) that they would be moving. When time came, they made the mistake of asking where they would like to live if they could make a wish. One shouted out, "I want to live by the zoo so I can visit the monkey cage every day." The other said, "No, I want to live with the fairies by the butterfly garden in the park, because they come out at night and I can stay up late to catch them." As you can imagine this verbal exchange became heated with each child believing that if they convinced their sibling to agree with them, their parents would fall in line. How disappointed they were to find out they were simply going to be moving five blocks away to a larger home.

Keep It Simple

The point that should not be missed in John's story is this: Children do not fully appreciate the logistics of moving. But if they are told factually exactly what the plans are *after* the plans have been made, they will find the best in the given situation. In other words, they simply want to know where they will hang their hats.

If your step-children are pre-school-age, you will have more flexibility in choosing a new location for the blended home. With older children, neighborhood schools and friends have already been established. If both you and your spouse each own a home, one or both of them will have to be sold or rented. If neither of the pre-owned residences is suitable for your blended family, another home will have to be purchased or rented. Before plunking down a fat deposit check, however, keep in mind that many states have restrictions as to the distance a biologic parent can move if they are the residential parent, or the parent with whom the children reside most of the time. That factor certainly must be considered before making any decisions; if this applies to you, don't forget to research the legality of your situation.

For the Step-Parent With No Biologic Children

If you are a step-parent with no biologic children, your decisions regarding choosing a residence may in many ways be simple. Some of you may be renting a home or apartment, or you may reside in a small home that offers no solutions for expansion to accommodate your blended family. Even if you think you could squeeze everyone in by rearranging rooms, turning a study into an extra bedroom for instance, don't forget to plan for storage and closet space, as well as the number of bathrooms that can accommodate the number of individuals in your blended family. Especially at "crunch time"—when everyone is scrambling to get ready for work and school—the bathroom is one area that cannot be overlooked. Also, since you have never "parented" before, you might be shocked to find out just how much "stuff" one child can accumulate, all of which they believe cannot be left behind.

If you already own a spacious home, but have no biologic children, and have decided to move your blended family into your residence, the square footage may not be the main problem, but that doesn't mean you have missed all the landmines. Living alone means that you have had the time to select furnishings and keep them in a certain manner. Without children to spill grape juice on the couch or leave crayons to melt on the patio table, you might be surprised at how quickly your beautiful furnishings can have that "used" look. If you are still up to the task, put away those items that are not replaceable, so that everyone is comfortable in their new surroundings.

Remember, aside from your bedroom, and perhaps your office space, every other square inch of your home will be occupied by your step-children and quickly considered to be public property. If you find that you are reluctant to "share" your things or your space, it is best to find a new residence where everyone begins on a level playing field. If you have chosen to keep your home because of your love of it, as a rental property, this also comes with some headaches, but they are not insurmountable. However, please go into your mental inventory and make certain that you are not keeping your home "in case" things don't work out; this signifies "red flags" that should not be dismissed without introspection, communication and resolution.

Certainly, as a step-parent, you also have the option of moving into the home previously occupied by your spouse and his or her ex. This may make the best sense logistically, so that your step-children's lives are not disrupted, but comes with its own set of unforeseen bumps. Remember, you will be moving into the home where your spouse and the former spouse lived; unless you have completely gutted and redecorated this home, there will be tell-tale signs of that marriage around every corner. Living with the ghost of a former spouse may not be as difficult on your spouse as it is on you, especially when it comes to the bedroom. If you are an individual who has absolutely no insecurities or unfounded jealousies, then by all means *go for it*. Otherwise, save everyone in the family the upset and seek out neutral housing.

Sara's Story

Sara simply didn't think she could spend even one more night living with the lingering presence of the former wife. Not only was the house still decorated in Anne's color palate and furnishings, but Sara's step-children didn't let her make a move without instructing, "Mommy says we should help ourselves at the dinner table; we don't want you to serve us"; or "When Mommy lived here we didn't have the Easter egg hunt in the front yard. She always made sure the bunny left the eggs in the house."

When Sara sought therapy, she arrived frustrated and angry, more so at her husband and step-children than the former wife. She believed Jake had never really transitioned from thinking of the house as his and Anne's; in fact, during a recent dinner party they hosted, he slipped and said, "My wife and I used to love entertaining in the dining room; the neighbors always had such a great time."

Sara felt a territorial need to make this home reflect her presence, but at the same time, she began to understand that these changes do not occur overnight. She knew that Jake had made the comment innocently, without realizing exactly what had been said. Still, after Jake and the children began to talk about the strangeness of seeing a woman who was not their mother peeling vegetables at the same spot at the sink, or talking on the phone and leaning against the same counter as their mother did, memories of the old days began colliding with the activities of their new step-mother. They all felt very badly about Sara's hurt feelings, and promised to make more of an effort to think before they spoke, but that didn't discount the unspoken thoughts that would undoubtedly haunt them for months, possibly years, to come.

When you move into the former marital home, it often feels to your step-children as though you are trying to replace their other biologic parent. Even if you are well-liked by them, a sense of disloyalty toward the other parent can arise. These images can be emotionally draining, and in young children without developed impulse control, they are likely to cause sadness or emotional outbursts.

Paradoxically, however, these same children who balk at having you step into the former marital home are often much less traumatized if their lives have not been uprooted and disrupted by a change in venue. The real answer to your housing dilemma will be based on a serious examination of financial and emotional considerations. You and your spouse are going to have to agree upon the best place to live after reviewing both the positive and negative aspects to this often convenient, but sometimes intrusive, decision.

For the Step-Parent With Biologic Children

Another scenario presents itself when you are a step-parent with biologic children whom you are blending with step-children. In this particular case, choosing a residence will have to incorporate the needs of everyone involved, including children at various stages of development and possibly in different school districts. This becomes much more difficult, because a move of this sort is going to impact those children who will leave their neighborhood schools and friends more than those children who will be less up-ended.

If all the children will be residing in the same home for the majority of time, the space requirement may increase dramatically. Ideally, it is best not to "buddy-up" children, expecting them to share rooms when they have never had to do so before. But if they must, then obviously this match will have to be age and gender appropriate. Unless your biologic and step-children are very young, under the age of six or seven for example, they will not appreciate bunking in with their new step-siblings. In fact, they would almost all prefer to have an extremely small room that belongs exclusively to them than to share a more spacious room. Sometimes a "private room" can be accomplished with a room divider, although even this division lends itself to problems as one child will have to walk through the bedroom of the other before reaching their destination. The story on page 128 is a good example of what can happen when families blend.

Housing for Permanents *and* Non-Permanents

Unless your children and step-children all reside permanently in the home, there will have to be other adjustments for the non-permanent residents. Most commonly, one set of children from

Billy and Fred's Story

Both Billy and Fred were thirteen years of age when their parents married. Billy, the biologic child of his father, Armand, had always lived in the home into which his step-mother Karen and her son Fred moved. Prior to this marriage, each had been an only child, and as such, did not have to share their bedroom, bathroom or games. In their former set-up their friends were welcome and had plenty of room to sprawl out when weekend sleepovers occurred.

However, in the six months since Armand and Karen wed, the boys spent most of their time bickering about who was responsible for trashing the room, or who lost the other's personal possessions. When the appointment was made for therapy, Fred had actually taken a can of white paint and painted a line down the center of the bedroom. This "vandalism" was the last straw for these very frazzled parents.

At first Fred refused to speak, but after the third session he finally started to communicate, although it was more like screaming and less like actually getting his point across. When he finally calmed down, he said, "I miss my old school and I miss my friends. I miss my house and I miss my dog. I hate that Billy doesn't want me in his room, and he makes it pretty clear that I am not wanted anywhere in the house. I hate my step-brother."

His outburst was quite disconcerting to his parents, but not unreasonable given the number of losses and adjustments that had to be made. Armand and Karen realized that they would have to give up some of their own space to redesign the study into a third bedroom. Once the division was complete, the boys began "visiting" each other in their rooms by invitation, rather than by default. As of this writing they have made great strides in bonding and making mutual friendships.

a parent, either biologic or step, lives in the home permanently, while the other set of children come to live on a temporary basis. This arrangement has its own set of problems in that the "permanent" children often resent having to share space with the "non-permanent" children. The permanent children tend to view their house, their space, their bathroom, their bedrooms, their toys and their food as just that … theirs! This makes the non-permanent children feel unwelcome and inferior, either having to fight for every inch of space or to cower in the background while their aggressive counterparts set up the rules.

Supervision Among Step-Siblings

If your blended family consists of biologic children of one gender and step-children of another, all of whom are reaching pubescence at about the same time, you have a recipe for disaster if there are not some strict ground rules and non-negotiable boundaries. Suffice it to say that none of these pre-teens or teens should be left to their own devices, for obvious reasons. If you don't know what these reasons are specifically, let's just say that they can be incorporated under the umbrella of "sexual experimentation."

These non-permanent-resident children should have their own space if at all possible. That space should include a dresser, closets, and a bed that belongs *only* to them. Without this sense of permanence and belonging, they feel as though they are a guest in their parent's house, rather than his or her child. It is up to you as the step-parent to insure that the permanent-resident children learn that they do not "own" the computer or the remote control, nor do they determine who is allowed to talk on the telephone and for what length of time. These boundaries cannot be worked out among the children themselves. Rather, free from hurtful accusations and bullying, an adult in authority must map out each and every aspect of their co-habitation.

The non-residential children deserve the same rights as the residential children, which are the rights that come with childhood. In case you aren't certain, those rights include:

- the right to feel safe
- the right to feel loved
- the right to not be threatened, frightened, bullied, or otherwise harassed by anyone
- the right to wake up happy and go to sleep peacefully.

Adulthood and all its problems are lurking just around the corner for your children. This is their only opportunity to be a kid. Non-permanent-resident children should not be "squeezed in" on the couch, or made to sleep on a blow-up mattress. Every child deserves a place to call home, even if home isn't where they live every single day.

Tom and Jason's Story

Joan and Tom had been married for less than one year, having both been married once before. They were conflicted between redesigning their family room into a bedroom for Tom's son who "visited" every other weekend, or simply purchasing an air mattress that could be inflated as necessary when it wasn't being stored downstairs in the basement. Although Tom believed Jason could make do with the inflatable bed, Jason's step-mother Joan disagreed. She thought it gave her children a clear message that Tom was "just the step-brother" and therefore was a lesser individual. Tom thought she was being ridiculous, so the couple decided to bring their problem to our office and abide by our decision.

Step-mother Joan provided more insight into Jason's feelings of exclusion. She overheard a conversation he had with a friend about not being able to invite him overnight because he did not have a bedroom. A second incident involved Jason needing an extra blanket on a cold night, but unable to locate one because he didn't know where the blankets were kept, as he was sleeping on the couch on the other side of the house. The fact that he didn't open closets to search for a blanket proved to Joan that he didn't feel comfortable nor did he feel like he belonged.

We agreed with Joan. It was more important that Jason felt like a member of a blended family than for the family to have a separate television room. It was agreed that Joan and Tom would use the formal living room on a more casual basis, placing a television and comfortable seating in place of the rigid formal couch. When the redesign was completed, Jason was thrilled to have his own bedroom, and almost immediately his step-siblings began including him more often. Within days Jason moved some personal possessions into his bedroom, so that when he spent time there he was surrounded by familiar items. The next time Jason spent the weekend with Joan and Tom, he planned a sleep-over with his best friend Matt.

Reminder To Be Kind

Now that you have a reasonable list of things to keep in mind when deciding on housing for your blended family, remember to try to be kind to the other biologic parent. Maintain a good working relationship. Someone is going to have to carpool the children between both homes, and it is entirely possible that you might just be that someone.

If your step-children are not old enough to drive, then the logistics of how they will depart from one parent's house to the other is usually worked out between the biologic parents with a definite schedule. However, schedules do not take into consideration unexpected events, such as one parent taking ill, or the automobile breaking down. At some point, *you* might be enlisted to offer assistance in transportation. If you have a good working relationship with the former spouse, your help will not only be appreciated, but it is yet another good example of positive role-modeling to your step-child.

Moving Day—A Family Celebration!

You can decide to make the transition as miserable or as exciting as your attitude dictates. All that packing and discarding, saving and tossing is backbreaking work, but since most children love an adventure, try to make this transition about the adventure rather than the work.

Since your clothing and household items will have to be sorted, this is a great opportunity to show the children first-hand the incredible happiness that giving to someone less fortunate brings. Allow the children to help with the decision to donate, and bring them with you when you give your items to charity. Congratulations! You have just made your first blended memory!

PART III: Honor Extended Family Members

When you are dealing with former extended family members there is the potential for a miserable mess. Emotions run high when families fall apart, and even higher when former family members feel their relationship with your step-children may be governed by you.

Put yourself in their shoes. It comes as no surprise that while you are not going to be listed in their "favorite friend" column initially, they assume that you are the "gate keeper" between them and your step-children. If they were thinking clearly, they would certainly put their best foot forward in the hope that they can influence you into granting access to the kids. However, common sense doesn't always abound during these emotional times, and often quite the opposite occurs. These people, with whom you may have never spoken, have already formulated opinions about you based upon their "co-conspirator," the other parent.

If you put yourself in their shoes, it will make it a little easier to recognize that any negative behavior on their part is based upon insecurity and fear of the unknown. Essentially, you hold all the cards if your step-children reside in your home, but even if they don't, any gatherings that you host on your step-children's behalf may or may not include the other biologic parent's friends or relatives based upon little more than your preference.

Grandparents

Grandparents, and time spent with them, are among children's fondest memories. That's good, because in a blended family there is always a surplus of grandparents! Your step-children do not want to be "divorced" from them, which is exactly how they will feel if they lose close contact with them. From the grandparent's perspective, their grandchildren are often the light of their lives; they also know that their time on earth is becoming shorter day by day.

Grandparents certainly will be able to interact with their grandchildren when they are staying with the other biologic parent, but suppose that your spouse and you have residential priority for your step-children; to these grandparents that translates into "we will hardly ever get to see our grandchildren again." Even worse, extended grandparents, like other relatives, don't always live close by, and for that reason alone, they cannot bear being unable to see their grandchildren for the full amount of time they will be visiting.

No one wants a friend or family member to experience divorce, but grandparents have an especially difficult time supporting their adult child, being torn from their son or daughter-in-law through divorce, and potentially losing the closeness of their grandchildren. As a step-parent, your schedule is very demanding, running your step-children to this appointment and that after-school activity, but your step-children's grandparents are often lonely and alone, hoping for current news and photos of their beloved grandchildren. It would be so special for these older folks, as well as your step-children, if you could try to include them in day-to-day news and special functions as often as you are able. We are all looking for areas to cut back on our busy lives, or at least schedule some events for a later date, but grandparents should not be one of those delayed events. They simply don't have that much time.

Bertha's Story

Bertha was always close to her six-year-old granddaughter, Amelia. She was present for her delivery into this world, and managed to come to every school play and birthday party, even though she was ailing. When her daughter Jane was served divorce papers, Bertha knew it wasn't John's fault that the marriage didn't last. Her daughter was just too irresponsible to take the institution of marriage and child-rearing seriously. John did the best he could to keep Bertha informed of school news, but because he held down two jobs, he no longer had as much free time to transport Bertha to her granddaughter's events. John was now a full-time single parent since his former wife moved away with another man, and he could barely get through the daily routines, never mind include Bertha.

By the time her granddaughter was eight years old, Bertha mostly "visited" by correspondence. Her diabetes was getting worse and she could no longer drive. Her granddaughter talked to her on the telephone at least once each week, but with their visits so few and far between, Bertha had the sense that she was losing her. When John told Bertha he was planning to remarry, Bertha cried. She knew there would never be room for her in their lives. She was wrong. John married a wonderful woman named Sue, who made it a point to introduce herself to Bertha by telephone. As soon as she understood the longing that Bertha had to see her granddaughter, Sue began making plans. Within three months Bertha was invited to visit for a long weekend, and within six months she was coaxed by Sue to move closer to the "family." Bertha's life was now complete because of this *stranger*—a new step-mother—who understood the importance of extended family.

The bottom line is this: Without exception, if you want to raise happy, emotionally-healthy, well-adjusted step-children, stand beside those individuals who have always been important in their lives.

One Big Happy Family

Like it or not, whether it is grandparents, aunts, uncles, cousins or close friends, these people do not want to disrupt your life, but neither are they willing to walk away from their grandchildren, nieces, nephews and friends simply because the parents were divorced. In Bertha's story there was a happy ending, but that is not always the case. When the water really gets murky is when the rest of the former biologic family rallies around the "suffering" parent, paying homage to their emotional wounds. Well-meaning relatives are torn between wanting a relationship with you, in order to be closer to your step-children, and fearing that if they are friendly, the other biologic parent will take their interactions as a form of treason, and possibly cut off all ties. Those ties, of course, include a relationship with the children, which cannot be jeopardized. Therefore, even though you are not the enemy, you may become the enemy by default. Because you can see the ripple effect of the undercurrent of former spouse/current spouse hostility, we advise you to revisit Strategy # 4 and try again to "make nice" to the former spouse for the sake of your step-children.

The degree to which the former extended family has access to your step-children is shared by you and your spouse. If you are in agreement, hosting them for the holidays or special events will certainly go a long way. You have no obligation to these individuals, but you do have a moral compass to do right by the children.

STRATEGY #7
Never Underestimate Your Importance

Regardless of how much you love your step-children, or the number of sacrifices you have made on their behalf, you will never be the biologic parent. Still, it doesn't diminish your importance in their lives. The label of "step-parent" is just that ... a label. It indicates a role, but does not detail the bond between you and your step-children, nor does it begin to define the impact you will have on the future of each one of them.

At the same time, your step-children may not fully comprehend your role in their lives until much later in their lives. However, none of them will mature without suddenly experiencing some type of epiphany of your importance.

In this chapter we share one story, but one that is significant enough to drive home a point that we hope you will never forget: *You make a difference every single day that you share with your step-children.* The simple act of carpooling, or cooking, or having a backyard barbeque will be remembered in detail when you least expect it. In some cases, your step-children may not verbalize their gratitude to you, but to others. This next story concerns Mayra, who was so caught up in her own life, as most teenagers are, that it was not until she became an adult that she realized the sacrifices made by her step-father because of his devotion to his family, and specifically his love for her.

This following tribute to a step-parent was found in our local newspaper. It was located in the Obituary section, dated July 2008, marking the one-year anniversary of the death of Jose Gonzalez. Its heartfelt message was written by his step-daughter, Mayra Pastrana-DeLuca.

```
In Memorial of Jose Gonzalez

Dad,

It's been exactly one year ago today
that you left this world to join
another. I am finally able to breathe
again without it hurting. I wanted you
to know that since the day you came
into my life it has been a blessing,
especially when you took the place
of my father who decided to walk away
from my mother and me. I still have
the first monopoly game you bought me
and we would play for days on end.
You also bought me my first record
player ... it was red and my first 45
record. The song was by Tom Jones,
"Green Eyed Lady," which I would play
over and over again. My first ballet
shoes. During my senior year in high
school you went with me shopping all
afternoon and bought me two of the
most beautiful dresses and shoes. You
walked me down the aisle twice. You
never once questioned or judged me on
any decision I ever made. You always
gave me unconditional love. I knew I
```

could count on you no matter when or
where. I never heard the word no. I
never told you any of these things when
you were here. I also never told you
how much I loved you. I just thought
you should know how proud I was to
be your daughter. They say blood is
thicker than water, well it isn't
true. I was fortunate to have you
in my life for thirty-eight years. I
will always love you.

—Mayra Pastrana-DeLuca

This dedication to her step-father is proof of his impact upon her life. We did not know Mayra personally, but we felt her anguish in her writing. It haunted us. We set out to meet the author of this remarkable anniversary-obituary. We found her almost immediately, in the most unlikely of circumstances, as if her step-father had a hand in easing her pain. The story marking the steps of our search, though almost unbelievable, is completely true. The events can be found on our web site, www.inthebestinterestofthechildren.com. Mayra was gracious enough to be interviewed and allowed us to use her story for this book.

Mayra's Story

"I am Puerto Rican. I tell you this not because of any superiority or inferiority to my ethnicity, but because it explains so much of my background. My family, of course, is Catholic. When my mother married my father, she was twenty-one years old, and he was only seventeen. My parents raised me strictly within the confines of our religion and our heritage. I was, for a long time, an only child. My father and I were very close, or so it seemed to me as a young child; my memories of him were laced with his sternness and his generosity. His pleasure was to bring me dogs, Chihuahuas, my substitute brothers and sisters.

In my home there was poverty; that is not to say we had no food. We did. But there was little money left after the essentials were purchased and the bills were paid. For me, I was rich. I had a mother and father and of course, my dogs. My father operated a *bodega*; inside was a bar and a pool hall. My mother was a seamstress, and did piece-work. They settled in New Jersey, although my father always spoke of going back to Puerto Rico. One day he did.

Although I was only six or seven years old, I remember my father very well during those days. I remember how happy I was when I was with him and how unhappy I was when at night I laid awake in bed and listened to my parents fight. Then one day, without notice, he came to me and said he was leaving. That was it. He picked up my dogs, told me good-by, and took them as he walked out the door.

My mother and I somehow made it even without any money from my father. I still went to Catholic school, and my mother sewed my uniforms each year. One of the nuns from the school, Sister Lillian, befriended us, and she may have been the reason I continued. When you are so little you do not know the financial picture, other than to know it was very hard for us. My mother kept our house immaculate; she worked to pay the bills. She was not a stupid woman, although she certainly never defied my father, yet she must have known something was going to come down. She saved some money and bought a car, something he did not allow her to have, and hid it some blocks away at a neighbor's house. When he walked out on us, at least she had the car.

My mother loved my father, even though he left us; I adored him. It was not easy for her. The Catholic community shunned us, assuming she must have done something to send him away. My mother had pride. She held her head up high, and she worked at the Bingo on the weekends. Sister Lillian made us feel welcomed, even when others did not.

Although we had no money, she always made sure to send me to Puerto Rico each summer to visit my father. I tried so hard to make him love me. Everything I did was for him; my school work, my stories, everything was for him to be proud of me. Then, when summer ended, I was sent back home to my grandparents where my mother and I lived. I counted the days until the next summer, until the next time I could try to make my father love me.

By the time I was ten or eleven years old, my mother began dating a friend of a friend of the family. He was ten years younger than my mother and had a paper route in our neighborhood when he was a boy. I remember when he first started coming around. I felt jealous. It was not that I didn't like him, but I didn't like how much time my mother spent with him. In those days, in my culture, you did not speak your mind; you respected your elders. That is what I did. My mother never asked if I minded Louie, that is the name he went by, and I never volunteered. Six months later they married.

Suddenly there was extra money in the house, not a lot, but enough that sometimes we did things. We played baseball, and games, and although he seemed strict, he was fun. I was cautious, not wanting to care about someone who might walk away. At first I called him "Dad" because he said I could, but then I decided to call him Louie, or Papa Louie, because calling him Dad didn't seem the right thing to do. I already had a dad. I remember one of his first talks with me; he said, "I'm going to be your dad. I will wear the pants in the family."

It wasn't long before I found myself in my teen years. He tried to guide me and I would say to him, "Don't tell me what to do, you're not my father." By the time I was fifteen, we had moved to Chicago; it was the best time of my life. There was so much to do, so much to see. The world opened up to me, and Louie made sure that I had what I needed. Then one day Louie announced that he and my mother were going to have a baby. I thought it was gross! I could not imagine my mother doing anything like that … having sex … getting pregnant.

He was in awe of the growing life inside her; he just beamed at the thought of it. He bought my mother the record, "Having My Baby" and played it over and over while he sang it around the house. Then my sister Sureida was born; we called her Sury, and I loved her! We all did. I continued to go to Puerto Rico each summer to win over my father, and each fall I came back home without much success.

Life continued; it was fun. Louie made sure that Sury and I had what we needed; it was as if our problems were behind us. Then our mother developed breast cancer. She died on the same year that Sury was only fifteen; my mother was fifty-two. Nothing was the same at home. Suddenly Louie had to take care of Sury, work, and grieve over his loss, and grieve he did. She was the love of his life, and when [Mom] died, you could see in his face that a part of him died with her.

I moved back into the house to help take care of Sury for awhile. Papa Louie finally began to meet some women to fill up his time and blot out his loneliness. It was as if he spent the next few years searching for my mother in everyone he met. One time I came back for a visit and he was dating a Cuban woman. I stopped in my tracks when I saw her; she was the spitting image of my mother. Still, he couldn't replace my mother. He never married again.

I married and divorced and married again. I had a son, Ryan. Sury grew up and had a child. One day I got a call on my cell phone. It was from a passer-by who had stopped at the scene of an accident on I-95 in Florida; she picked up a cell phone and went through the listings until she found my number and called me. The cell phone belonged to the victim of the accident. The cell phone belonged to Louie.

I called my husband and together we went to a nearby hospital where the ambulance had taken Louie. Others arrived; they knew that Louie went to the aid of a fellow worker whose battery died on the highway. On his way to help him, Louie's tire exploded and his truck rolled several times before coming to a stop. The doctors and nurses worked on him for two hours. [When I learned that he died] I asked to please let me be with him. They didn't want to, but I had to see him no matter *what* he looked like. When I walked in he was still warm; he had a wonderful smell about him, a Louie smell I always loved. But it was his face that I will never forget. For the first time since my mother died, his face looked like the old Louie, a happy Louie, a Louie who had finally found peace. It was as if he was saying to me, "I'm home now, you can let me go."

It was the day after my birthday that Louie died. For one whole year I could not think of anything else; I spent so much time and energy trying to prove myself to my real father, trying to be whatever would make him love me. I never realized everything I ever needed was right beside me all the time. It was Louie. It was always Louie.

I needed to find a way to express how much he meant to me. All I could think of was writing a letter to him on the first year anniversary of his death; I just wanted someone to know. I wanted someone to read it in his honor. I wished the message could get to him somehow.

❖   **Message Received.**   ❖

STRATEGY #8
Get the Help You Need

Everyone can use assistance at some time in their lives. Whether that assistance comes from confiding in a good friend, researching information from the Internet, shopping for appropriate book titles that address issues that you are experiencing, seeking professional help, or even soliciting legal intervention, do not hesitate to reach out! Difficulties that are not quickly identified and resolved turn into larger problems which fester. If you have unanswered questions, feel frustrated with situations that seem as if they are beyond your control, or simply want to vent your feelings, you owe it to yourself to do something about it.

If you believe that you or your family members are not adjusting as they should, please be pro-active in your decision to seek professional help. That is what family therapists and psychologists who specialize in family dynamics do best; they mend fractured families. Your problem is unique to you, but it is not unique to professionals who are adept at sizing up situations and offering decisive remedies for improvement.

Blending families is not easy. Even if everyone does the best they can, there is always another opinion from another vantage point that can give that missing ingredient to make a good family even better. Seek help from psychologists, parent-coaches, parent-support groups or even television shows (such as *The Nanny*), for tips on getting control of your family one behavior at a time.

Many useful parenting books, as well as books on relationships are available; so check out the family section of your local bookstores, as well as libraries and the Internet. One-size does not fit all, or in other words, seek advice from an author whose values and standards seem most similar to your own. There is a treasure-trove of literature on family dynamics, and within those pages, are the answers to your questions. Good luck!

In this chapter we will highlight signs or situations that may indicate a need for outside help. We hope you will realize that you are not unique in your difficulties, and that many step-parents, just like you, have admitted that they couldn't do it alone.

When *You* Need Help

Signs or situations indicating that *you* need help:
1. Consistent feelings of anger, irritability or agitation
2. Consistently feeling that you are "alone" in your own family
3. Generally feeling that you are unappreciated or disrespected
4. Almost always feeling that the brunt of responsibilities fall upon your shoulders
5. Generally feeling that your spouse's expectations of you are unreasonable
6. Regularly experiencing angry verbal outbursts
7. Often experiencing crying spells and feeling "blue"
8. Consistently wishing you could turn back to a time before you married
9. Regularly having thoughts of leaving your spouse
10. Constantly wishing your step-children were gone from your life.

If you are consistently/regularly experiencing any of the above, your step-children may not like you because you may be displaying traits that make you unlikable. They are always looking for signs of stability, trust, consistency and non-judgmental support. Introspection often reveals behavior that may be inadvertently sabotaging your own happiness. As well, questions may be swirling in your head, causing a shift in your ability to focus clearly on specific problems.

In order to ascertain exactly what is wrong, and what measures can be taken to improve the situation, take a good look at the common missteps discussed below: about inadequate parenting skills, emotional stamina, wanting to quit, etc. If any of these issues resonate with you, and add to your insecurity, anger, or frustration, you would benefit greatly from outside help.

Note that your spouse may be experiencing these feelings as well. He or she will exhibit the same types of behavior that you have, and should be encouraged to identify and talk openly about their feelings without fear of retribution or emotional upheaval. This is not the time to invite your spouse to discuss important issues, only to personalize his or her feelings. Your spouse can love you very much, but still feel overwhelmed or angry by the enormity of the emotional burden of family responsibility.

Commonsense Advice for Common Missteps in Step-Parenting

1. If your parenting skills are really undeveloped. Most of you may be unreasonably hard on yourselves on this item. It is a rare parent who believes that he or she hits the mark successfully on parenting, but there is certainly always room for improvement. Parenting is dynamic; it is always evolving as the needs of the adults and children grow and change. There are many Parenting Support Groups, as well as information about parenting in books and through the Internet for specific questions.

But in general, discussions with other parents or step-parents provide comparative experiences and helpful hints that can be quite adequate. With severe problems that include the entire family, a psychologist who specializes in family therapy would be the first line of defense. If the difficulties center around one member of the family, such as a teenage step-child, a parenting coach is often the perfect solution. They can be found by searching the Internet for "Parent Coaches" and including the name of your state or closest city.

2. If your emotional stamina is taxed too heavily. If you are feeling stressed, it may help you to remember that you are not alone. The pressures of everyday life are enormous, and anything additional tips the scales into burnout. There are several things you can do to ease your emotional burdens: delegate responsibilities, talk about your problems with friends—venting does wonders to release built-up pressure, schedule your personal time and stamp it in cement, make time for romance and emotional sharing with your spouse.

3. If you want to quit the family. Think about this decision very carefully! There may be times when it is very tempting to "throw in the towel," rather than expend the energy to work things out. But often, what feels like an insurmountable problem can be dissected into very workable action steps. Sometimes looking at a problem in its totality is overwhelming, but when it is chipped at bit by bit, the solution seems closer. This is where therapy can really identify and help to resolve situations. However, if you decide that you really cannot be a member of this family any longer, please try to leave with dignity, with civility, and with as little damage to the other family members as possible.

4. If you really don't like your step-children. There is so much for you to like about your step-children; beneath their sometimes crusty exterior are just confused, frightened, lonely kids who need a hug, symbolically speaking. Once you get to know them, you may find that you are surprised at how great they really are! This will work for most of you, but not all of you. If you still do not like your step-children, after examining your own emotional suitcases as well as theirs, it is really urgent that you go to individual and/or family therapy to try to resolve these issues. However, if you continue to dislike them to the degree that you can't even pretend to care about them, it is our opinion that not only will you be better off without them, but they will be better off without you.

We can't impress these sentiments strongly enough. If you truly do not want to be in the company of your step-children, if you feel secretly pleased when they are miserable, if you go out of your way to find fault with them and wish them harm or wish them gone, then do everyone a favor and leave first.

Love is elusive; it cannot be measured nor explained. It cannot be wished for or wished away. It is the mainstay of relationships and the strength that creates lifelong bonds. If you find you *do not* and *cannot* love your step-children, you are not a horrible person; but with that knowledge comes the understanding that you now have the responsibility to do the right thing.

5. If your step-children really don't like you. As we've noted throughout, many children sorely lack manners or boundaries. If they have been less than supervised, if their boundaries have been blurred, if their behavior is accepted regardless of respect and attitude problems, then they certainly will perceive that *you*, as an outside adult, will be less likely to tolerate these infractions. At the least, they fear that you will influence their parent(s) to take charge, and at worst, that you will take charge yourself. In other words, you have suddenly taken the form of a speed bump on their otherwise smooth, albeit risky, road toward autonomy.

In another scenario, perhaps they believe that there is something questionable or objectionable with you, and are merely trying to protect their biologic parent from a lifetime of living with the wrong person. We understand that their parent's partner choice is not their call, but we are dealing with children and their immature reasoning systems. Leslie's children were a perfect example of that.

Leslie's Story

When Leslie's husband died, he left a one-million-dollar life insurance policy. It was no surprise that, a couple of years following his death, she was besieged by suitors. After all, she was beautiful, talented, kind and rich. Her teenage boys were skeptical of every suitor she dated, convinced that these men were only after her money. Finally, after three years of dating, Leslie met a wonderful man and fell in love. Their courtship would have been like a Hollywood storybook romance, except for the constant interference by her children, and their contempt of Robert.

Robert was an ideal step-parent. He had already raised his biologic children and was experienced with teenage boys. He took them to their baseball practice, purchased skateboards for their birthdays, and even surprised them with a trip to a new skateboard park. But the more he tried to get close to the boys, the more distant the relationship turned, until Leslie called for an appointment for family therapy.

It wasn't long before the boys confessed their suspicions of a "hidden agenda" even though there was no such evidence, and that they secretly really liked Robert. Nonetheless, they believed it was their job, in their father's absence, to protect their mother. As it turned out, Robert had quite a bit of money of his own, and was quite financially secure. Although he was advised against divulging that information, he was asked to be perfectly honest with his step-sons about his prior failed marriage and the love he held for Leslie. The more he entrusted his true feelings to them, the more they trusted him.

Leslie and Robert have now been married for over five years, and the boys look forward to coming home from college as often as possible to enjoy "family activities" together.

Two Valuable Books

There are many resources available to assist you in parenting, not only through various stages of child development, but also throughout difficult times—such as the process and aftermath of divorce. Our two previous books offer simple but important information which, if followed, will change the dynamics of your family, whether splintered or whole.

In our first book, *In The Best Interest Of the Child, A Manual for Divorcing Parents*, we explain exactly what is going on in the minds of your children as their parents muddle their way through the legal labyrinth of the divorce process. It includes basic information on child-rearing, including what to expect from children of all ages, how to set boundaries, how to enforce consequences, when to be concerned about those emotional behaviors that are normal and not so normal, how to protect your children from the fallout of divorce, and how to continue to parent with a united front from two separate households.

Our second book, *You Don't Know Anything, A Manual for Parenting Your Teenager*, uncovers the intrinsic issues that present themselves to all pre-teens, teens and young adults, giving their parents a front row seat to the drama of why kids do what they do. It further details how to stay one step ahead of your teens to keep them safe and happy. Again, this book explains what can be reasonably expected from teenagers, as well as the specifics for setting their boundaries and enforcing consequences without you falling victim to feelings of helplessness that so often plague parents whose children are marching toward independence.

6. If you are jealous of your step-children. If a step-parent is feeling jealous over the attention a child is receiving, unless that attention is disproportionate, the step-parent is asking for trouble. No biologic parent should be placed in a position to choose, but if they are, then they had better choose their children! It gives pause to think about how immature it is to envy a child who has been mired in divorce muck only to now find themselves embroiled in step-parenting jealousy. If this is your situation, however, admitting it honestly is the first step. Seeking professional help should be a close second.

7. If money issues are jeopardizing relationships. Jealousy insinuates envy of attention, but it can also include factors such as finances, and specifically the amount of money your spouse doles out to your step-children. Money is shared in some manner in a marriage, even if accounts are kept separate. Ultimately, marital money, regardless of what "pot" it goes into, still affects both adults, so when one party seems to be spending lavishly on children while the other party wants to create financially independent young adults, there is going to be resentment if a compromise cannot be reached. If salaries are put in one martial pot, one of you may feel that some of your hard-earned money is being spent frivolously on the children. However, to be fair, children do seem to need an enormous amount of money to keep them in clothing, school supplies, extra-curricular activities, sports, hobbies, and most of all FOOD! The best case scenario is that your step-children are responsible and conscientious enough that they not only achieve excellent academic grades, but also hold down a good-paying after-school and weekend job. In reality, however, the most that can be hoped for is that there is at least a part-time job that puts gas in their car and gives them weekend spending money. If not, they will still need the gas in their cars and weekend spending money, and they will probably need it from the marital money pot.

Claire's Story

Claire didn't make any excuses for her anger; she said she was sick and tired of her teenage step-son's reckless spending and their father's enabling attitude. Roy worked two jobs to make sure his kids had everything, including automobiles, cell phones, computers, clothing and the latest electronics. Claire's biologic children were grown, but during their formative years she made sure that they worked for everything they wanted. She said it "disgusted" her to see the money given away so freely.

Roy didn't dispute that he enjoyed purchasing big ticket items for his sons, not only because he wanted them to keep up with the other kids in town, but also because he could well afford to spoil them. He defended his sons by stating that they were both excellent students and if they took on a part time job it would take away from their studies.

Both Claire and Roy made some good points, but with their philosophical differences, compromise would not come easily. In therapy they were both given a budget to run the household, with the leftover money split between them to use in any way that pleased them. Claire saved her money, while Roy continued to lavish his boys with it.

As a point of interest, although this division of family money was considered to be fair by both of them, Claire continued to harbor resentment at her husband's inability to stop spending; although she agreed that it was his money to do with as he pleased, what pleased him did not please her. As of this writing, Claire and Roy have decided to separate.

Whether you are in a blended family or not, money differences can cause irreparable damage and anger; in the above case, both parents were unwilling to compromise with their actual spending or saving habits, and no amount of "fair division" would bring them together philosophically.

If money differences are causing the big problems in your family you can make several improvements to ease the tension. Sit down with your spouse and make a budget, including "mad money" which is for no other reason than personal choices. If there isn't enough "mad money" to divvy up, cut back on something else until there is. Everyone needs to have pocket money for incidentals and shouldn't have to get permission to make a small, personal purchase.

Decide with your spouse what activities are important to set aside money for as a family. If the kids love skating, for example, perhaps they can rent skates to accommodate their growing tootsies, but admission to the skate park should be slated and put aside. Refreshments can be a thermos of hot chocolate and some sandwiches, rather than the refreshment stand.

Neither parent should be fully "responsible" for paying the bills; this invites resentment on the part of the person paying the bills because, as we all know, finding the money to pay bills is a great big headache. It also invites resentment on the part of the parent not paying the bills, who may constantly question "where did all the money go?" Set aside a bi-monthly bill-paying schedule where both of you sit down together to forge through this unpleasant but necessary task.

Give reasonable amounts of money to the children, but divided fairly and age-appropriately. Certainly the monetary needs of a five-year-old child are not the same as a thirteen-year-old child; but there's no doubt about it … kids need things and things cost money.

If you begin this quest knowing the exact dollar amount you have to work with, it won't be such a surprise when you have to reach into your pocket. Most of all, keep a financial log. At the end of the day, mark down all the "extras" that were not anticipated, such as payment for a lost library book, or a parking ticket. Then, at the end of the month, it will make much more sense to both of you as to where your hard-earned dollars went, and which purchases do not have to be duplicated in the future.

By the way, if your child's carelessness cost you ten dollars for the lost library book, this is something your "kitty" should be reimbursed, as they "work it off" by doing extra chores around the house. They will be much less likely to make the same mistake twice!

Serious financial woes should be addressed with credit counselors. These are difficult economic times, but even in the best of situations, with the most responsible adults, budgeting takes a backseat to overspending. There is no shame in recognizing that your money matters may be somewhat off track. This is unfortunately a common occurrence. But, denying that the problem exists, or being too embarrassed to seek advice, some people close their eyes and hope the problem will correct itself. It won't!

Each month, both partners should set aside some time to reassess the budget; monetary situations, like life, are dynamic, and change constantly. By having monthly meetings, the safeguard is that both partners remain aware of any impending issues, and work together as a team to solve them. If money problems cannot be solved with your best efforts, or emotions escalate every time the issue of money is brought up, a financial counselor can assess your needs and goals to set you back on track.

6. If your spouse is sabotaging your efforts. When problems crop up in a biologic family, members come together to identify and resolve problems. When things go wrong in a blended family there is often an undercurrent of suspicion or resentment, with members blaming each other. Family members look toward the step-parent as the villain more often than the savior.

Spouses who sabotage your attempts at step-parenting by allowing or even encouraging your step-children to disrespect or disobey you are seriously undermining your authority. Such behaviors may have some deep-seated psychological issues which should be dealt with in family therapy. Tyler certainly tried to put Wanda in just this type of situation.

7. If you or your spouse decide to end the marriage. Sometimes marriages fail. Even when you and your step-children have made tremendous positive adjustments that are firmly rooted in love and trust, this may not be enough to hold a marriage together. Those very same children, who in the past had caused you so much self-doubt and tears because you didn't know if you could ever love them, may now be causing you anguish because you can't imagine ever leaving them. You worry about them with good reason; they have already been put through one divorce, and now may soon be victims of another. You do not want to cause them pain. But if after soul-searching, marriage counseling, and compromise you believe with all your heart that you cannot remain in your marriage, then there is no reason to allow a bad situation to become worse.

Tyler's Story

After Tyler and Wanda were married he made one thing clear to her; his children (two female adolescents) were "his" children and he would decide what rules they had to follow. Unfortunately Tyler didn't have any rules established, and he more or less took a back-seat to parenting while setting Wanda up to be the "heavy."

One night when the girls disregarded their curfew by one hour, Wanda implemented the Behavior Chart and told them they were both grounded for the following weekend. The girls laughed at her, and Tyler joined in as well.

When the weekend came, Tyler told the girls behind Wanda's back, "Don't tell your step-mother but as soon as she leaves to go into town, you can sneak out for a few hours." Wanda might not have known about all the times that Tyler went behind her back to undermine her authority, but she found out about this one. She sat down with the girls and told them the importance of respecting her decisions. It was then that the oldest girl said, "Daddy says it doesn't matter what you say, he will just let us out of it."

In family therapy we confronted Tyler with these statements, which he admitted were accurate. In fact, he found them amusing at Wanda's expense. When we suggested he and Wanda come in for some parenting sessions, he refused saying, "I work hard enough. I'm not going to spend my free time listening to somebody telling me what I can and can't do."

Unfortunately, someone *did* tell Tyler what to do; it was a judge who instructed him that his daughters were picked up for drunk driving. Wanda wasn't present for that lecture; Wanda was once again single.

Whether you will file for divorce and whether that divorce will be contested, there will be many unknown factors. You will have to divide housing and property, money and assets. Most of all, you will have to "divide" children. Much as you might wish to remain in contact with your step-children, that will be at the discretion of their biologic parent(s) unless the children are of age to make those decisions for themselves.

One thing is certain: these children cannot afford any further chaos. If you and your spouse cannot come to a mutual decision regarding your continued contact with the children, you do not have the right to manipulate them for your own gain. If you have decided to leave the marriage, part of that marriage was your step-children.

When Your Children or Step-Children Need Help

1. If your step-children are in jeopardy. There is one exception to walking away from your current relationship—that is, if you have any knowledge that places your step-children in jeopardy if they remain with their biologic parent. You need to do something about this situation *before* you make your exit. Specifically, we are referring to emotional, physical or sexual aggression against your step-children. If that type of activity has occurred or is occurring, as a step-parent you have a duty to protect your step-children.

Emotional Abuse

Emotional abuse includes verbal threats, insults, bullying or any other infliction of emotional pain. This cannot be measured by the naked eye but nonetheless leaves lifelong scars on its victims. It is inflicted purposefully by an immature coward for the sole purpose of causing pain.

Physical Abuse

Physical abuse is the attempt to control an individual through physical aggression either for purposes of intimidation and/or fear, and includes a strike, bruise, punch, slap, body slam, shove or kick. This type of abuse may or may not involve an object such as a belt or other household item turned weapon. Physical abuse is a cowardly act made upon an innocent child who is unable to protect themselves; its purpose is to control the individual through physical pain and humiliation.

Sexual Abuse

Sexual abuse is perhaps the most heinous of all abuse, and includes inappropriate touching, groping, sexual innuendos, or any sexual act upon the child for the purpose of power, control, humiliation or perverted sexual gratification. There is no such thing as a "mistake" of a perpetrator in sexual abuse; even one instance is the forerunner of further escalation, regardless of apologies or alleged remorse. Sexual abuse leaves permanent, invisible scars to a child's body and soul.

If there is any doubt in your mind that without your watchful eye your step-children are in danger of abuse, you have a moral obligation to notify the other biologic parent and the authorities.

You must not walk out on them without first securing their safety. Knowledge cannot be erased; neither can child abuse.

2. If your children or step-children are genuinely unhappy. When there are difficulties in a marriage, often the adults are so consumed with their own issues that they give little thought to what their step-children are going through. Depression and anxiety, once thought to be disorders of adults, are now widely acknowledged as leaving no gender or age unscathed. Children have quite a bit to be worried about. They have to perform well academically; they are learning how to be socially responsible; they are wondering where they will fit in, who will be their friends, what their future holds and how they will get there. The one thing they weren't counting on was that there would be internal problems within your marriage that would spill over into their lives. These children have already lived through one divided family, and they may now be faced with another. It is likely that they will react either by becoming introverted and withdrawn, or angry and hostile. If unaddressed, these feelings will not simply resolve themselves. Everything children are subjected to becomes an indelible life experience. When your marriage is rocky, their feelings of trust, betrayal and hopelessness are on the edge. When they exhibit signs of ongoing unhappiness, seek professional help (family therapy) for yourself, your partner, and particularly for your children.

3. When your children or step-children are seriously acting out—breaking the law ... etc. Children, even from the most stable of families, may have their own internal turmoil, which they often act out in destructive ways. Alcohol or drug use and vandalism are common behaviors that teens and young adults turn to when they are confused, angry and left to their own devices. If your children or step-children have difficulty obeying rules and regulations, beginning with the social rules of your household and extending to the rules of society, these traits cannot be minimized as "That's a kid for you!" Children who act out, in even one destructive act, must be taken seriously. Whether the issue is low self-esteem or underlying rage, they should be taken to a child psychologist specializing in behavioral issues. Although some acting out is to be expected, behavior that is consistently negative, hostile, aggressive and purposeful spills over into a category of behavior that should be evaluated and probably treated by family counseling sessions. If you wait until your child "grows out of it," the problem will undoubtedly take on a life of its own. If there is chaos and turmoil in your home, either because of arguments, isolation, or underlying hostility in the family, these problems must be sorted out and treated in order to put children back on a functional path.

When *Your Spouse* Needs Help

Your spouse may also be exhibiting signs that he or she is not happy. This might show up in agitation or outright anger, in avoidance of home and responsibilities, like making late night appointments or activities excluding the family.

If there are difficulties that can be sorted out through open communication, you might initiate a time to sit down with your spouse to talk. If his or her unhappiness manifests in a manner that appears to be beyond your scope to understand or handle, you might suggest that they seek professional counseling. Below are some guidelines to consider:

1. If your spouse is angry, encourage him or her to make an appointment with a psychologist who specializes in anger management issues.
2. If your spouse is not behaving in a stable manner, notify the other biologic parent if you suspect that his or her children are in danger.
3. If your spouse makes threats, notify authorities if you feel imminent danger.

4. Call your local family services agency; in our area (Florida) it is known as The Division of Children and Families. These agencies can be found in your local phone directory, or by calling 911 for emergency assistance.
5. Whenever possible, follow through on any strategies for helping yourself or others before you leave the marriage and family relationship. If you must leave, follow through as well as you can.
6. If you suspect abuse, especially sexual in nature toward the children, you have a legal duty and moral obligation to protect those children by eliciting help from all of the above immediately.

RESOURCES

I. Internet Resources

Websites
There are so many sites on the World Wide Web that come under the umbrella heading of "Step-parenting," with more sites being added daily. There is no shortage of information on groups, chat rooms, newsletters and even on-line counseling for blended families. We will list a few of these sites which have either come under the heading of "Step-parenting" or "Blended Families" on Google.
- **www.stepsforstepmothers.com**: a website created by step-mothers for step-mothers
- **www.stepfamilysuccess.com**: a site for step-parents and blended family coaching.
- **www.newstepparents.com**

Online Magazines / Essays / Articles
There are also magazines available on the Internet, better known as e-zines, as well as essays and articles posted again under the heading "Step-parents" on Google. We recommend the following:
- "All Things Step-Parenting," an article by Karon Goodman
- *Blended Families*, a free newsletter for those who register

- Blended Family Resource Center, based in Redmond, Washington, with posted articles.
- *Bonus Families*, questions and answers written by professionals.
- "The Evil Step-Mother," an essay by Maureen F. McHugh on her experience with her step-son.
- "Help Your Teen Adjust to a Step-Family," articles and advice given by various authors.
- "The Influence of Grandparents and Step-Grandparents on Grandchildren," an article published by North Dakota State University, author Laura DeHaon.
- Loretta Mosca's articles about step-parenting and blended families.

Agencies and Associations
- **Step-Carefully**, an organization that publishes a newsletter and offers online counseling.
- **Step-Parenting Survival Company**, survival secrets and workshops.

II. Counseling and Advice via Phone

Listed below are several groups that offer their expertise according to individual needs:
- **Step-Family Foundation**, telephone and in-person counseling, 212-877-3244.
- **The Step Family Network**, includes lists of state-by-state resources and support groups for step-families, 1-800-487-1073.

Immediate Assistance

The following list is a quick reference guide for issues that need immediate assistance:

- **24-hour Emergency Hotline**: emergency or drug overdose: 911
- **Abandoned Infant Hotline**: 1-866-505-7253
- **Adolescent Resources Parent Hotline**: 1-800-400-0900
- **Alcohol and Other Drug Services**: 1-800-565-7450
- **Alcohol and Substance Abuse Services**: 1-800-553-5790
- **Association of Anorexia Nervosa and Associated Eating Disorders**: 1-800-762-7402
- **Banking; Consumer Info and Complaints**: 1-877-226-5697
- **Child Protective Services**: 1-800-565-4304
- **Crime Stoppers**: 1-800-255-1301
- **Daycare Complaint Hotline**: 1-800-732-5207
- **The Coffee House Emergency Shelter for Teens**: 1-800-544-3299 or 1-800-546-3432
- **The Drop Inn**: 1-800 568-4415
- **Gambling Information**: 1-800-437-1611
- **HIV Information and Testing**: 1-800-565-4620
- **HIV Nightline 5 P.M.-5 A.M. daily**: 1-800-273-2437
- **Missing and Exploited Children**: 1-800-FIND-KID
- **National Youth Crisis Hotline**: 1-800-448-4663
- **Positive Images (Gay and Lesbian)**: 1-800-579-4947
- **Pregnancy Counseling Center**: 1-800-575-9000
- **QUEST** (Intensive out-patient program for eating disorders): 1-800-284-2162
- **Rape Hotline**: 1-800-545-7273
- **Social Advocates for Youth Emergency**: 1-800-544-3299
- **United Against Sexual Assault**: 1-800-545-7270
- **YWCA Domestic Violence Hotline**: 1-800-546-1234

BIBLIOGRAPHY

- Baksh, Nadir and Laurie Murphy. *In The Best Interest Of The Child, A Manual for Divorcing Parents*, Prescott, Arizona: Hohm Press, 2007.
- Baksh, Nadir and Laurie Murphy. *You Don't Know Anything, A Manual for Parenting Your Teenager,* Prescott, Arizona: Hohm Press, 2009.
- Beavais-Godwin, Lauren and Raymond Godwin. *The Complete Adoption Book.* Avon, Massachusetts: Adams Media, 2005.
- Barnes, Bob. *Winning the Heart of Your Step-Child.* Grand Rapids, Michigan: Zondervan, 1997.
- Fay, Jim and Foster W Cline. *Secrets of Step-Parenting.* Golden, Colorado: Love and Logic Press, 1994.
- Freud, Sigmund. *The Interpretation of Dreams.* New York: Barnes and Noble Classics, 2005.
- Harris, Bonnie. *Confident Parents, Remarkable Kids.* Avon, Massachusetts: Adams Media, 2008.
- Hill, E.D. *I'm Not Your Friend, I'm Your Parent.* Nashville, Tennessee: Thomas Nelson, 2008.
- Lutz, Erica. *The Complete Idiot's Guide to Step-Parenting.* New York, New York: Simon Schuster MacMillan Company, 1998.

INDEX

OTHER TITLES OF INTEREST FROM HOHM PRESS

IN THE BEST INTEREST OF THE CHILD
A Manual for Divorcing Parents
by Nadir Baksh, Psy.D. and Laurie Murphy, R.N., Ph.D.

This book will help parents save their children unnecessary anguish throughout the divorce process. The authors have a private practice with families and also work as court-appointed evaluators in child-custody disputes. Their advice and direction is eminently practical – detailing what adults can expect from a custody battle; what they will encounter in themselves and in their children (emotionally, physically, mentally) during divorce; advising how parents can make sense out of children's questions; offering guidance in making decisions for themselves and their kids; and explaining the ultimate importance of putting the child's needs first.

Paper, 144 pages, 6 x 9 inches, $16.95   ISBN: 978-1-890772-73-4

YOU DON'T KNOW ANYTHING ... !
A Manual for Parenting Your Teenagers
by Nadir Baksh, Psy.D. and Laurie Murphy, R.N., Ph.D.

This book offers immediate and clear help to parents, family members and teachers who are angry, confused, frustrated, sad, or at their wit's end in dealing with their teenagers. Beyond advice for crisis situations, *You Don't Know Anything ...!* informs parents of the new stresses their kids today must cope with, and suggests ways to minimize these pressures for both adults and teens. Patience, caring, vigilance, "street smarts," knowledge of the teenage brain – these are among the many skills that parents today need. The book points the way to those skills, and encourages parents and other adults to resume their legitimate roles in teens' lives.

Paper, 188 pages, $12.95   ISBN: 978-1-890772-82-6

To Order: 800-381-2700, or visit our website, www.hohmpress.com

CONSCIOUS PARENTING
by Lee Lozowick

Any individual who cares for children needs to attend to the essential message of this book: that the first two years are the most crucial time in a child's education and development, and that children learn to be healthy and "whole" by living with healthy, whole adults.

Offers practical guidance and help for anyone who wishes to bring greater consciousness to every aspect of childraising, including: * conception, pregnancy and birth * emotional development * language usage * role modeling: the mother's role, the father's role * the exposure to various influences * establishing workable boundaries * the choices we make on behalf on our children's education ... and much more. *Publisher's Seconds are available at a reduced price.*

Paper, 378 pages, $17.95.   ISBN: 978-0-934252-67-6

PARENTING, A SACRED TASK
10 Basics of Conscious Childraising
by Karuna Fedorschak

Moving beyond our own self-centered focus and into the realm of generosity and expansive love is the core of spiritual practice. This book can help us to make that move. It highlights 10 basic elements that every parent can use to meet the everyday demands of childraising. Turning that natural duty into a sacred task is what this book is about. Topics include: love, attention, boundaries, food, touch, help and humor.

"There is no more rigorous path to spiritual development than that of being a parent. Thank you to Karuna Fedorschak for reminding us that parenting is a sacred task." – Peggy O'Mara, Editor and Publisher, *Mothering Magazine.*

Paper, 158 pages, $12.95   ISBN: 978-1-890772-30-7

To Order: 800-381-2700, or visit our website, www.hohmpress.com

THE ACTIVE CREATIVE CHILD
Parenting in Perpetual Motion
by Stephanie Vlahov

Active/creative children are often misunderstood by the medical community, by schools, and by their own parents. Their energy is astounding; their inquisitiveness is boundless. Channeling that energy is not only helpful, but necessary. Supporting that inquisitiveness is essential! This book provides specific hints for coping, for establishing realistic boundaries, and for avoiding labels and easy judgments where any child is concerned. Written in a simple, journalistic style, the author draws from her experience with her two active/creative sons, and those of others, to present a handbook of encouragement and genuine help.

Paper, 105 pages, $9.95   ISBN: 978-1-890772-47-5

TO TOUCH IS TO LIVE
The Need for Genuine Affection in an Impersonal World
by Mariana Caplan
Foreword by Ashley Montagu

The vastly impersonal nature of contemporary culture, supported by massive child abuse and neglect, and reinforced by growing techno-fascination are robbing us of our humanity. The author takes issue with the trends of the day that are mostly overlooked as being "progressive" or harmless, showing how these trends are actually undermining genuine affection and love. This uncompromising and inspiring work offers positive solutions for countering the effects of the growing depersonalization of our times.

"An important book that brings to the forefront the fundamentals of a healthy world. We must all touch more." – Patch Adams, M.D.

Paper, 272 pages, $19.95   ISBN: 978-1-890772-24-6

To Order: 800-381-2700, or visit our website, www.hohmpress.com

DIVINE DUALITY
The Power of Reconciliation between Women and Men
by William Keepin, Ph.D., with Cynthia Brix, M.Div.
and Molly Dwyer, Ph.D.

This book demonstrates a revolutionary type of healing work between men and women, known as "gender reconciliation." Based on 15+ years of development, this process has created remarkable results within groups as diverse as nuns and priests in the Catholic Church, and most recently with members of the South African Parliament. The creative and compassionate methods designed by the author and his team at the Satyana Institute (of Freeland, Washington) take a broad leap beyond other approaches that are more oriented to addressing the needs of the couple. No other book currently deals with this subject with the depth of insight and proven results presented here.

Paper, 320 pages, $16.95   ISBN: 978-1-890772-74-1

STAINLESS HEART
The Wisdom of Remorse
by Clelia Vahni

Anyone who has ever felt guilt will find both comfort and direction in this clearly written and compassionate book. The "stainless heart" is Clelia Vahni's description of the pure, essential nature of the human being. This heart, however, is rarely touched. One reason for this impasse, the author states, is that we have built walls around the heart, out of shame; or have held ourselves apart so we don't get hurt anymore (or hurt others) because we are afraid of the pain that guilt carries. Guilt is different from genuine remorse, the author argues. Guilt destroys us, while true remorse is the entry into truth, to a clear vision of life "as it is," and thus to a transformed relationship to ourselves and others.

Paper, 160 pages, $12.95   ISBN: 978-1-890772-40-6

To Order: 800-381-2700, or visit our website, www.hohmpress.com

RADIANT JOY BRILLIANT LOVE
Secrets for Creating an Extraordinary Life
and Profound Intimacy with Your Partner
by Clinton Callahan

This hard-hitting and innovative book about man-woman relation-ship immediately challenges the deceptions about love and intimacy rampant in today's patriarchal culture. At the same time, *Radiant Joy Brilliant Love* reveals a step-by-step process for discovering and living out alternative possibilities.

The author claims that even the "best" of our relationships are still generally basic level; what he calls "Ordinary Human Relationship." He asserts that two more domains remain to be explored: namely, Extraordinary Human Relationship and Archetypal Love. The book shows exactly how to enter these new domains, and how to stay there long enough to cultivate genuine intimacy, nurturance, excitement and satisfaction together.

Paper, 576 pages, $29.95   ISBN: 978-1-890772-72-7

THE JUMP INTO LIFE
Moving Beyond Fear
by Arnaud Desjardins
Foreword by Richard Moss, M.D.

"Say Yes to life," the author continually invites in this welcome guide-book to the spiritual path. For anyone who has ever felt oppressed by the life-negative seriousness of religion, this book is a timely antidote. In language that translates the complex to the obvious, Desjardins applies his simple teaching of happiness and gratitude to a broad range of weighty topics, including: sexuality and intimate relationships, structuring an "inner life," the relief of suffering, and overcoming fear.

Paper, 278 pages, $12.95   ISBN: 978-0-934252-42-3

To Order: 800-381-2700, or visit our website, www.hohmpress.com

WHEN SONS AND DAUGHTERS CHOOSE
ALTERNATIVE LIFESTYLES
by Mariana Caplan

A guidebook for families in building workable relationships based on trust and mutual respect, despite the fears and concerns brought on by differences in lifestyle. Practical advice on what to do when sons and daughters (brothers, sisters, grandchildren ...) join communes, go to gurus, follow rock bands around the country, marry outside their race or within their own gender, or embrace a religious belief that is alien to that of parents and family.

"Recommended for all public libraries."—*Library Journal.*

Paper, 264 pages, $14.95   ISBN: 978-0-934252-69-0

THE WAY OF FAILURE
Winning Through Losing
by Mariana Caplan

This straight-talking and strongly inspirational book looks failure directly in the face, unmasking it for what it really is. Mariana Caplan tells us to how to meet failure on its own field, how to learn its twists and turns, as well as its illusions and realities. Only then, she advises, is one equipped to engage failure as a means of ultimate "winning," and in a way that far exceeds our culturally-defined visions of success.

Paper, 144 pages, $14.95   ISBN: 978-1-890772-10-9

To Order: 800-381-2700, or visit our website, www.hohmpress.com

About the Authors

Nadir Baksh, Psy.D. is a Licensed Clinical Psychologist specializing in Clinical and Forensic Psychology since 1984. He is a Fellow of the American Association of Integrative Medicine and the American Board of Forensic Examiners, and Diplomate of the American Psychotherapy Association, with over twenty-two years of clinical experience in office practice. Dr. Baksh is considered an expert in court testimony, and has worked for twenty years in child custody evaluations and marital therapy. He sees first hand the effects of separation and divorce on the individuals in the relationship, especially the children. He is coauthor with Laurie Murphy of *In the Best Interest of the Child: A Manual for Divorcing Parents* (Hohm Press, 2007) and *You Don't Know Anything …!: A Manual for Parenting Your Teenagers* (Hohm Press, 2008).

Laurie Elizabeth Murphy, R.N., Ph.D. has raised four children. Since the beginning of her training in 1968 she has worked with patients and families. For the past twenty years she has specifically focused on a clinical practice dealing with marital issues, divorce and its impact on children. She is coauthor with Nadir Baksh of *In the Best Interest of the Child: A Manual for Divorcing Parents* (Hohm Press, 2007) and *You Don't Know Anything …!: A Manual for Parenting Your Teenagers* (Hohm Press, 2008).

Contact Information

Laurie Murphy and Nadir Baksh have an active website. Please visit them at www.InTheBestInterestOfTheChildren.com. Use the *Contact Us* section on the website to send your questions, and they will try to answer as many as possible. They also love comments from readers. Send correspondence to 421 Martin Avenue, Stuart, Florida 34996.